MARK OF THE BEAR

LEGEND AND LORE OF AN AMERICAN ICON

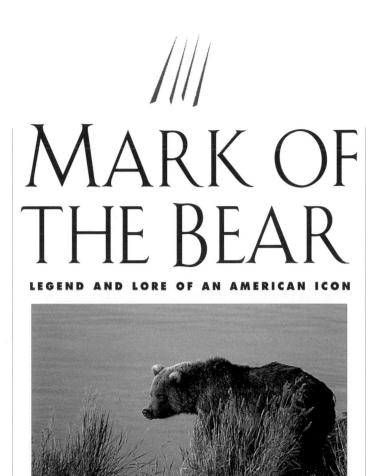

EDITED BY PAUL SCHULLERY

PHOTOGRAPHS BY
JEFF FOOTT, THOMAS MANGELSEN, AND TOM AND PAT LEESON

SIERRA CLUB BOOKS

A TEHABI BOOK

Rick Bass, "My Grizzly Story," first appearing in *Audubon* magazine, January-February 1996. Reprinted in this abridged form with permission by Rick Bass.

Frank Dufresne, "The Twenty-fifth Bear," an excerpt from *No Room for Bears* by Frank Dufresne. Holt, Rinehart and Winston, New York. Copyright © 1965 by Frank Dufresne. Reprinted with permission by Harold Ober Associates and the heirs of Frank Dufresne.

Barry Lopez, "Tôrnârssuk: Ursus maritimus," a chapter from *Arctic Dreams* by Barry Lopez. Charles Scribner's Sons, New York. Copyright © 1986 by Barry Holstun Lopez. Reprinted by permission of Sterling Lord Literistics, Inc.

Doug Peacock, "The Black Grizzly," an excerpt from *Grizzly Years*, by Doug Peacock. Henry Holt & Company, New York. Copyright © 1990 by Doug Peacock. Reprinted in this abridged form with permission by the author.

Theodore Roosevelt (1858-1919), "Old Ephraim," an excerpt from *Hunting Trips of a Ranchman*. G. P. Putnam's Sons, New York, 1885.

Ernest Thompson Seton (1860-1946), "Wahb," an abridged excerpt from *Biography of a Grizzly*. The Century Company. Copyright © 1899 by Ernest Thompson Seton.

Library of Congress Cataloging-in-Publication Data
Mark of the bear / edited by Paul Schullery.
   p.   cm.
   ISBN 0-87156-903-5 (cloth: alk. paper)
   1. Bears—North America—Anecdotes 2. Bears—North America—Folklore.   I. Schullery, Paul.
   QL737.C27M33   1996
   599.74'446—dc20   96-17650
                             CIP

Mark of the Bear was conceived and produced by Tehabi Books.
Nancy Cash–*Managing Editor;* Laura Georgakakos–*Manuscript Editor;* Kathi George-*Copy Proofer;* Sam Lewis–*Art Director;* Andy Lewis–*Art Director;* Tom Lewis–*Editorial and Design Director;* Sharon Lewis–*Controller;* Chris Capen–*President.*

Sierra Club Books and Tehabi Books, in association with The Basic Foundation, a not-for-profit organization whose primary mission is reforestation, will facilitate the planting of two trees for every one tree used in the manufacture of this book. This edition is printed on acid-free paper that meets the American National Standards Institute Z39.48 Standard.

Printed in Hong Kong through Mandarin Offset. First edition 1996   10 9 8 7 6 5 4 3 2 1

Page 1:   *For all our time spent looking at bears, we'll never know what they're thinking when they look back at us.*

Page 2-3:   *During their first two years of life, brown bear cubs look to their mother to teach them most of what they will need to know to survive .*

Page 4-5:   *It is speculated that the grizzly bear evolved into the assertive animal it is when it moved out of the refuge of forest and into open ground.*

Page 6:   *Bears are fond of water, whether searching for fish or cooling off on a hot day.*

CONTENTS

FOR THE
LOVE OF BEARS

TODAY THE BEAR IS AN abstraction for most of us, which is reason enough to present a collection of stories like *Mark of the Bear*. These stories are written by people who have taken bears personally, people who have spent enough time in bear country to form something deeper than mere impressions of bears they've seen. By bringing the bear back to a personal level—by at least vicariously sharing in encounters—perhaps we can appreciate a little more deeply how good it is to have bears around. These writers have emerged from their time in bear country—the Arctic, the high West, New England, or whatever wild corner of the country they've traveled—with something amounting to a viewpoint, even a position, on this whole complicated business of being with bears.

I call it a complicated business, and others may agree, but unless we extend our bear appreciation beyond where bears actually live, we just have no idea how complicated the bear is. Unless we pursue the bear through literature, lore, and spiritual traditions, we can't guess what a fantastic world of dreams and ideas the people who preceeded us constructed as they met, fought, and wondered about bears. The mythologist Joseph Campbell has written that Neanderthal bear-skull sanctuaries in Old World caves are "our earliest evidence anywhere on earth of the veneration of a divine being." This is an almost breathtaking revelation: the bear was a primary presence in early human religion (and if you've met one, it's not hard to understand why). We turned to it even before we found our way to the huge variety of

The adult grizzly's massive skull anchors tremendously strong jaw muscles, so strong that they can crush buffalo bones or bite through a metal skillet.

superhuman and supernatural deities that peopled the world's later belief systems.

Nor did the power of the bear fade when all these later belief systems flourished. Human ecologist Paul Shepard says that "the bear is the most significant animal in the history of metaphysics in the northern hemisphere." Indeed, Shepard maintains that even when humans became largely urban and lost touch with wild landscapes, they didn't really leave the bear behind; they simply brought it along in subtle, even subconscious forms, so that it haunts us as an image and an idea, somehow all the more powerful for being so remote. An endless string of modern fictional, animated, and commercial characters, all the way from Pooh, Paddington, Teddy, Yogi, and Smokey to the modern horde of care bears and gummy bears, seem to indicate that Shepard knows what he's talking about. We are still reinventing the bear, reinventions full of intellectual tangles and twists that have transformed one of the world's great carnivores into, among other things, a sweet-natured baby-voiced toy, a symbol of industrial forestry, and a logo for countless ski resorts, bars, and other human enterprises. And we will most likely continue to find new ways to imagine the bear.

Still, there's nothing like a real bear, one you can watch and hear and even smell as it goes about its bear business. The writers in this book have all hunted their share of imagined bears in the books, lore, and oral traditions of many societies. But what distinguishes these writers is that they have also, to one extent or another, found their way back to a more immediate relationship with the bear. They read and listened and learned, but then they went out and found a real bear.

And what a variety of bears they found. For some, like Roosevelt, the real bear reveals itself in good part through what he's been told by other, more experienced bear watchers, both from his own and other cultures. For other writers, most especially Seton, the bear's own perspective is imagined, adding a new dimension to the vast canon of bear lore. Seton's bears achieve their power for us partly through caricature and humanization, and partly through the underlying truth of their lives, of which he was an avid and renowned student. For others, the bear still represents something primally threatening: violence, or at least the possibility of violence, has always been an essential element of our idea of the bear. Both people and bears die in this book.

An important component of the bear's complexity is its physical remoteness. For most of these writers, the bear reveals itself grudgingly, in quick unforgettable glimpses that linger and tantalize us. I have likened bear watching to fishing; as the saying goes, so often the cast, so seldom the strike. I would hate to compute a bears-per-hour sighting average for the time I've spent out there looking for them, because I am sure it would be so many hours-per-bear instead. Much if not most of our fascination with bears must have to do with the overwhelming majority of the time we spend anticipating and then remembering the sight of one. The bear reveals itself more as a forceful presence than as a visible object, demanding from us an awareness of its occupation of the neighborhood even when there's no sign of it around. Whatever learning or ignorance we may bring to our search for the bear, when we meet one we are immediately set off on a new hunt.

Much as we may hope to encounter the bear, it is through

such encounters that the abstract bear can become abruptly and painfully real. One of the great ironies of our relationship with bears is that, for all the excitement and conversational mileage we may get from our meetings with them, and as much as we may want to find them, if we truly care for the animal we will try very hard to avoid such encounters. Bears do all they can to avoid us, and along busy trails it is probable that for every actual encounter in which people are aware of the bear's presence, the bear avoids dozens of others. The greater the number of encounters, especially ones in which the bear has been surprised and feels threatened, the greater the chance of injury to the person, and an injured person is always bad for the bears. So even if you are willing to take that risk on your own behalf, remember that you are also taking it on behalf of the bear.

The writers of this collection share a passion for the bear and for the world the bear inhabits, a passion that has compelled all of them to speak and to work on its behalf. I know that hunting is increasingly unfashionable, but no one did more for bears than that most famous of American hunters, Theodore Roosevelt, whose conservation policies set America on a course of saving the large wild areas bears so desperately need to survive. What is less appreciated about Roosevelt is that he wrote a book's-worth of excellent natural history and adventure stories about bears, the best contribution to our understanding of bears up to that time.

Seton, too, through his many popular books and articles, as well as his leadership in youth education, is an enduring force in nature appreciation. He was an enormously popular writer in the early years of this century, and produced both light natural history and encyclopedic reference works. I suspect that his *Biography of a*

Grizzly, from which his excerpt is taken, is the best-selling bear book of all time (it is a tribute to the complexity of the bear's image that if the *Biography* has been outsold, it is probably by A. A. Milne's *Winnie-the-Pooh*).

Likewise Frank Dufresne, longtime Alaskan and former director of the Alaska Game Commission, worked both as a professional manager and a writer to champion admiration for and protection of bears. His excellent book *No Room For Bears* was one of the first, if not the first, volumes directly devoted to the crisis in bear conservation. With such a rich experience in the bear's world, Dufresne knew both the mythic richness and the sometimes jarring reality of getting along with bears, and portrays them both here.

The rest of the writers represented here have followed in that tradition of writing about the bear to honor it and ensure its future. I won't venture to predict where we each will stand eventually as conservationists—we can only dream of having an effect of the likes of Roosevelt's or Seton's—but I will assert that we're working hard at it, in our own ways and from our own disciplines.

When I read the essays of Roosevelt, Seton, and Dufresne, and even more when I read the essays of Bass, Lopez, Schmidt, Spragg, Ehrlich, and Peacock, I am struck by what conservation has come to mean in the modern world. It is much more than the saving of wild places and wild creatures. It is the saving of the many relationships that human culture has developed with those places and creatures. What this book celebrates is our coming to terms with the bear, in all the ways we find to do that. It celebrates a whole galaxy of impulses, emotions, ideas, and hopes we may experience whenever we see the mark of the bear. ////

In the polar bear the Arctic landscape has created the perfect amphibious predator—powerful, far-ranging and at home in the planet's harshest environment.

The surprise we feel at seeing a bear standing upright on its hind legs is the recognition of their jarringly humanlike stance.

The bear's sense of smell is legendary—even reputable scientists claim to have observed bears picking up the scent of a carcass ten miles away.

In spite of their massive paws, bears are adept even at digging up small clams.

EXCERPTED FROM *GRIZZLY BEAR* BY
ERNEST THOMPSON SETON

WAHB

WAHB'S THIRD SUMMER HAD brought him the stature of a large-sized Bear, though not nearly the bulk and power that in time were his. He was very light-colored now, and this was why Spahwat, a Shoshone Indian who more than once hunted him, called him the Whitebear, or Wahb.

Spahwat was a good hunter, and as soon as he saw the rubbing-tree on the Upper Meteetsee he knew that he was on the range of a big Grizzly. He bushwhacked the whole valley, and spent many days before he found a chance to shoot; then Wahb got a stinging flesh-wound in the shoulder. He growled horribly, but it had seemed to take the fight out of him; he scrambled up the valley and over the lower hills till he reached a quiet haunt, where he lay down.

His knowledge of healing was wholly instinctive.

He licked the wound and all around it, and sought to be quiet. The licking removed the dirt, and by massage reduced the inflammation, and it plastered the hair down as a sort of dressing over the wound to keep out the air, dirt, and microbes. There could be no better treatment.

But the Indian was on his trail. Before long the smell warned Wahb that a foe was coming, so he quietly climbed farther up the mountain to another resting-place. But again he sensed the Indian's approach, and made off. Several times this happened, and at length there was a second shot and another galling wound. Wahb was furious now. There was nothing that really frightened him but that horrible odor of man, iron, and guns, that he remembered from the day when he lost his Mother; but now all fear of these left him. He heaved

Overall massiveness and a pronounced shoulder hump are two of the features that help distinguish grizzly bears from black bears.

painfully up the mountain again, and along under a six-foot ledge, then up and back to the top of the bank, where he lay flat. On came the Indian, armed with knife and gun; deftly, swiftly keeping on the trail; gloating joyfully over each bloody print that meant such anguish to the hunted Bear. Straight up the slide of broken rock he came, where Wahb, ferocious with pain, was waiting on the ledge. On sneaked the dogged hunter; his eye still scanned the bloody slots or swept the woods ahead, but never was raised to glance above the ledge. And Wahb, as he saw this shape of Death relentless on his track, and smelled the hated smell, poised his bulk at heavy cost upon his quivering, mangled arm, there held until the proper instant came, then to his sound arm's matchless native force he added all the weight of desperate hate as down he struck one fearful, crushing blow. The Indian sank without a cry, and then dropped out of sight. Wahb rose, and sought again a quiet nook where he might nurse his wounds. Thus he learned that one must fight for peace; for he never saw that Indian again, and he had time to rest and recover.

The years went on as before, except that each winter Wahb slept less soundly, and each spring he came out earlier and was a bigger Grizzly, with fewer enemies that dared to face him. When his sixth year came he was a very big, strong, sullen Bear, with neither friendship nor love in his life since that evil day on the Lower Piney.

No one ever heard of Wahb's mate. No one believes that he ever had one. The love-season of Bears came and went year after year, but left him alone in his prime as he had been in his youth. It is not good for a Bear to be alone; it is bad for him in every way. His habitual moroseness grew with his strength, and any one chancing to meet him now would have called him a dangerous Grizzly.

He had lived in the Meteetsee Valley since first he betook himself there, and his character had been shaped by many little adventures with traps and his wild rivals of the mountains. But there was none of the latter that he now feared and he knew enough to avoid the first, for that penetrating odor of man and iron was a never-failing warning, especially after an experience which befell him in his sixth year.

His ever-reliable nose told him that there was a dead Elk down among the timber.

He went up the wind, and there, sure enough, was the great delicious carcass, already torn open at the very best place. True, there was that terrible man-and-iron taint, but it was so slight and the feast so tempting that after circling around and inspecting the carcass from his eight feet of stature, as he stood erect, he went cautiously forward, and at once was caught by his left paw in an enormous Bear-trap. He roared with pain and slashed about in a fury. But this was no Beaver-trap; it was a big forty-pound Bear-catcher, and he was surely caught.

Wahb fairly foamed with rage, and madly grit his teeth upon the trap. Then he remembered his former experiences. He placed the trap between his hind legs, with a hind paw on each spring, and pressed down with all his weight. But it was not enough. He dragged off the trap and its clog, and went clanking up the mountain. Again and again he tried to free his foot, but in vain, till he came where a great trunk crossed the trail a few feet from the ground. By chance, or happy thought, he reared again under this and made a new attempt. With a hind foot on each spring and his mighty shoulders underneath the tree, he bore down with his titanic strength: the great steel springs gave way, the jaws relaxed, and he tore out his foot. So Wahb was free again, though he left behind a great toe which had been nearly severed by the first snap of the steel.

Again Wahb had a painful wound to nurse, and as he was a left-handed Bear,—that is, when he wished to turn a rock over he stood on the right paw and turned with the left,—one result of this disablement was to rob him for a time of all those dainty foods that are found under rocks or logs. The wound healed at last, but he never forgot that experience, and thenceforth the pungent smell of man and iron, even without the gun smell, never failed to enrage him.

Many experiences had taught him that it is better to run if he only smelled the hunter or heard him far away, but to fight desperately if the man was close at hand. And the cow-boys soon came to know that the Upper Meteetsee was the range of a Bear that was better let alone.

One day after a long absence Wahb came into the lower part of his range, and saw to his surprise one of the wooden dens that men make for themselves. As he came around to get the wind, he sensed the taint that never failed to infuriate him now, and a moment later he heard a loud bang and felt a stinging shock in his left hind leg, the old stiff leg. He wheeled about, in time to see a man running toward the new-made shanty. Had the shot been in his shoulder Wahb would have been helpless, but it was not.

Mighty arms that could toss pine logs like broomsticks, paws that with one tap could crush the biggest Bull upon the range, claws that could tear huge slabs of rock from the mountainside—what was even the deadly rifle to them!

When the man's partner came home that night he found him on the reddened shanty floor. The bloody trail from outside and a shaky, scribbled note on the back of a paper novel told the tale.

It was Wahb done it. I seen him by the spring and wounded him. I tried to git on the shanty, but he ketched me. My God, how I suffer! JACK.

It was all fair. The man had invaded the Bear's country, had tried to take the Bear's life, and had lost his own. But Jack's partner swore he would kill that Bear.

He took up the trail and followed it up the cañon, and there bushwhacked and hunted day after day. He put out baits and traps, and at length one day he heard a *crash, clatter, thump*, and a huge rock bounded down a bank into a wood, scaring out a couple of deer that floated away like thistle-down. Miller thought at first that it was a land-slide; but he soon knew that it was Wahb that had rolled the boulder over merely for the sake of two or three ants beneath it.

The wind had not betrayed him, so on peering through the bush Miller saw the great Bear as he fed, favoring his left hind leg and growling sullenly to himself at a fresh twinge of pain. Miller steadied himself, and thought, "Here goes a finisher or a dead miss." He gave a sharp whistle, the Bear stopped every move, and, as he stood with ears acock, the man fired at his head.

But at that moment the great shaggy head moved, only an infuriating scratch was given, the smoke betrayed the man's place, and the Grizzly made savage, three-legged haste to catch his foe.

Miller dropped his gun and swung lightly into a tree, the only large one near. Wahb raged in vain against the trunk. He tore off the bark with his teeth and claws; but Miller was safe beyond his reach. For fully four hours the Grizzly watched, then gave it up, and slowly went off into the bushes till lost to view. Miller watched him from the tree, and afterward waited nearly an hour to be sure that the Bear was gone. He then slipped to the ground, got his gun, and set out for camp. But Wahb was cunning; he had only *seemed* to go away, and then had sneaked back quietly to watch. As soon as the man was away from the tree, too far to return, Wahb dashed after him. In spite of his wounds the Bear could move the faster. Within a quarter of a mile—well, Wahb did just what the man had sworn to do to him.

Long afterward his friends found the gun and enough to tell the tale.

The claim-shanty on the Meteetsee fell to pieces. It never again was used, for no man cared to enter a country that had but few allurements to offset its evident curse of ill luck, and where such a terrible Grizzly was always on the war-path.

Then they found good gold on the Upper Meteetsee. Miners came in pairs and wandered through the peaks, rooting up the ground and spoiling the little streams—grizzly old men mostly, that had lived their lives in the mountain and were themselves slowly turning into Grizzly Bears; digging and grubbing everywhere, not for good, wholesome roots, but for that shiny yellow sand that they could not eat; living the lives of Grizzlies, asking nothing but to be let alone to dig.

They seemed to understand Grizzly Wahb. The first time they met, Wahb reared up on his hind legs, and the wicked green lightnings began to twinkle in his small eyes. . . . Wahb was about to charge, but something held him back—a something that had no reference to his senses, that was felt only when they were still; a something that in Bear and Man is wiser than his wisdom, and that points the way at every doubtful fork in the dim and winding trail.

Of course Wahb did not understand what the men said, but he did feel that there was something different here. The smell of man and iron was there, but not of that maddening kind, and he missed the pungent odor that even yet brought back the dark days of his cubhood.

The men did not move, so Wahb rumbled a subterranean growl, dropped down on his four feet, and went on.

Late the same year Wahb ran across the red-nosed Black-bear. How that Bear did keep on shrinking! Wahb could have hurled him across the Graybull with one tap now.

But the Blackbear did not mean to let him try. He hustled his fat, podgy body up a tree at a rate that made him puff. Wahb reached up nine feet from the ground, and with one rake of his huge claws tore off the bark clear to the shining white wood and down nearly to the ground; and the Blackbear shivered and whimpered with terror as the scraping of those awful claws ran up the trunk and up his spine in a way that was horribly suggestive.

What was it that the sight of the Blackbear stirred in Wahb? Was it memories of the Upper Piney, long forgotten; thoughts of a woodland rich in food?

Wahb left him trembling up there as high as he could get,

and without any very clear purpose swung along the upper benches of the Meteetsee down to the Graybull, around the foot of the Rimrock Mountain; on, till hours later he found himself in the timber-tangle of the Lower Piney, and among the berries and ants of the old times.

He had forgotten what a fine land the Piney was: plenty of food, no miners to spoil the streams, no hunters to keep an eye on, and no mosquitoes or flies, but plenty of open, sunny glades and sheltering woods, backed up by high, straight cliffs to turn the colder winds.

There were, moreover, no resident Grizzlies, no signs even of passing travelers, and the Blackbears that were in possession did not count.

Wahb was well pleased. He rolled his vast bulk in an old Buffalo-wallow, and rearing up against a tree where the Piney Cañon quits the Graybull Cañon, he left on it his mark fully eight feet from the ground.

In the days that followed he wandered farther and farther up among the rugged spurs of the Shoshones, and took possession as he went. He found the sign-boards of several Blackbears, and if they were small dead trees he sent them crashing to earth with a drive of his giant paw. If they were green he put his own mark over the other mark, and made it clearer by slashing the bark with the great pickaxes that grew on his toes.

The Upper Piney had so long been a Blackbear range that the Squirrels had ceased storing their harvest in hollow trees, and were now using the spaces under flat rocks, where the Blackbears could not get at them; so Wahb found this a land of plenty: every fourth or fifth rock in the pine woods was the roof of a Squirrel or Chipmunk granary, and when he turned it over, if the little owner were there, Wahb did not scruple to flatten him with his paw and devour him as an agreeable relish to his own provisions.

And wherever Wahb went he put up his sign-board:

Trespassers beware!

It was written on the trees as high up as he could reach, and every one that came by understood that the scent of it and the hair in it were those of the great Grizzly Wahb.

If his Mother had lived to train him, Wahb would have known that a good range in spring may be a bad one in summer. Wahb found out by years of experience that a total change with the seasons is best. In the early spring the Cattle and Elk ranges, with their winter-killed carcasses, offer a bountiful feast. In early summer the best forage is on the warm hillsides where the quamash and the Indian turnip grow. In late summer the berry-bushes along the river-flat are laden with fruit, and in autumn the pine woods gave good chances to fatten for the winter. So he added to his range each year. He not only cleared out the Blackbears from the Piney and the Meteetsee, but he went over the Divide and killed that old fellow that had once chased him out of the Warhouse Valley. And, more than that, he held what he had won, for he broke up a camp of tenderfeet that were looking for a ranch location on the Middle Meteetsee; he stampeded their horses, and made general smash of the camp. And so all the animals, including man, came to know that the whole range from Frank's Peak to the Shoshone spurs was the proper domain of a king well able to defend it, and the name of that king was Meteetsee Wahb.

Not easily distracted from fishing, a scent on the wind will quickly bring a bear to full attention.

It is a tribute to the adaptability of bears that they can make themselves at home in so many landscapes.

Most hikers are unaware of a bear's presence, though often the bear is watching them.

An early snowfall can sometimes surprise even a seasoned bear.

Following pages: **A**laskan salmon streams are among the few places in nature where bears overcome their usual unsociable nature and spend time in large groups.

AN ORIGINAL ESSAY BY

PAUL SCHULLERY

MARK OF THE BEAR

THE BEAR STORIES WE MOST LOVE to tell are about meetings. I was climbing the mountain and suddenly there was a bear—all I had ever imagined, more than I could ever understand. It worked its way up a distant slope, it emerged from the forest, it rose from behind a huge log, it ambled up the trail toward me, it materialized in plain view where an instant before there had been nothing. Encounters with this disturbingly familiar yet achingly remote animal are and always will be at the center of our bear lore.

But for every hour I spend watching bears I spend many hours wandering around bear country looking for them. None of the time spent looking is wasted, because every moment I am out there I am in the presence of bears. I search for that presence as eagerly as I search for the animals themselves. I am aware of the presence of hundreds of past generations of bears. Ultimate omnivores, their masterful foraging has led them over every trail, every meadow, every ridge, countless times before my arrival and I know they are there.

They are there in every rollable stone that I see, each promising bear treats underneath—a juicy beetle, some crickets still stiff and slow in the morning shade, a few succulent new shoots of grass. The same bear that will practically wallow in a deer or elk carcass becomes a fine, precise diner on these dainties. I've encountered so many freshly rolled rocks over the years that I no longer consider them stationary elements of the landscape. Realizing how bears engage in landscape redesign leads one to other

Bears have their own opinions about our presence in their territory.

awakenings. Those long front claws that make attacks so dreadful have a more important purpose—digging. So much of what bears like to eat is underground that they have become skilled and determined treasure hunters. They dig for all kinds of bulbs and roots, some so small it's a wonder their metabolisms can justify the effort. Here in the West, they dig out the dried plant caches of pocket gophers, the pocket gopher himself a tasty by-product of the work. They dig out marmot dens and ground squirrel burrows. In a single day a big bear might coarsely till a huge patch of meadow and the next day may move two tons of soil and rock on a slope, spreading it in a long fan down the hillside below.

We tend to think of beavers as the only real ecological engineers of the wilderness but beavers work only in the narrow bottoms of drainages. Bears are at it everywhere. Walk a trail in grizzly country and notice not only the holes where bears have gone after some rodent but, more chillingly, the raw parallel claw marks along the edge of the hole. The churning of all that soil, wherever it comes to rest, affects many other lives, from the rodents the bear was seeking to the millions of microorganisms and dozens of plant species always on the lookout for fresh habitats to colonize. So bears are not merely mammalian rototillers, they are inadvertent gardeners as well.

Where I live, the occasional Douglas fir may live several centuries, but most of the trees don't last that long. And when they do die, one of the many things that may hasten their decay is the bear, astride the fallen trunk, those powerful shoulders hunched and straining as the claws pull long furrows in the bug-rich wood. But trees that are still alive give us the greatest aware-

ness of bear presence. Bear folklore has few more cherished notions than the "bear tree," a sort of ursine signpost and bulletin board, which bears use to signify something; just what it signifies has been debated by naturalists for many years. It certainly has to do with communication or so many wouldn't choose the same tree.

What I spend the most time looking for, is what tracking expert James Halfpenny has cleverly described as "bear art"—the marks bears make when they actually climb the tree. Our best local tree for showing this is the aspen; its soft white bark is easily punctured and beautiful black scars form wherever branches have fallen, or birds have poked through, or bears have climbed. It is my favorite reminder of the neighborhood bears because once they have climbed the tree, their "art" is there forever. Aspen are fewer than 1 percent of the trees in Yellowstone, so they don't begin to register the number of times bears have climbed trees, but they're the easiest to read, so I always watch for them. There are few aspen groves anywhere around here that don't have at least one tree with a set of claw marks from the base up to thirty feet, and some even extend to the more spindly high trunk. Just yesterday, a short snowshoe hike of half a mile turned up half a dozen of these trees, each with its own unique set of signatures.

Each begs to have its story told. Was this a drama of a bigger bear, perhaps a grizzly, chasing a smaller one, and the smaller one taking refuge in the tree? Often the claw marks are not four or five neat black dots, but are instead a row of curving lines, the bear having slipped a few inches or even a foot in its haste. Or was this just a cautious mama black bear sending her cubs up to safety until she investigated suspicious sounds nearby?

For the presence of today's bears, I look for the newest marks: signs on the ground. This search begins in early spring, when the first of the grizzly bears—the big males—roust themselves from their dens to go in search of food and mates. In April and May, I've stood at the snow line at 8,000 feet and aimed my spotting scope at white ridges a thousand feet higher, ridges whose deep drifts were plowed aside by the passage of big bears on the march. Few things that grizzly bears do give me as great a sense of their irresistible mass as the broad, deep ditches they leave in snow so dense that I would be unable to move through it at all.

After the snow is gone and the ground dries and hardens, I'm more likely to find tracks in streambeds where a bear stepped into soft mud. I keep looking for tracks then, but I'm far more likely to come upon scat. Call it droppings, feces, dung, or just poop, bear scat is one of the great attention getters of the wilderness. A quick examination reveals many things about the bear: what it was eating (we dissect scat the way students disassemble frogs, and we learn even more), how long ago it was here (even if the scat is old and dry, you shouldn't assume that its source is necessarily far away), and how big it is (there's at least a rough correlation between diameter of scat and diameter of bear).

I once came upon a big pile of berry scat so fresh that it was still settling; the juices were just beginning to run across the trail. This was no abstraction, and for the first time I fully realized the extent to which I am routinely in the presence of bears. They are probably much closer more often than I'd care to know.

To us, feces is just something to be disposed of as quickly as possible, but to a bear it's an important calling card. I once saw the tracks of a large male grizzly bear who was following a female; every time she defecated he defecated right on top of hers; this was no casual act, and probably made a very persuasive territorial statement to any other bears nearby. Everything that gives scent or leaves evidence that might serve the bear is put to use at times. They live in a world not only of visible signs but of scent and sound as well.

One wet spring day in Glacier National Park, a biologist friend and I hiked over a pass known at that time to have a lot of bear activity, both grizzly and black. We made noise constantly, not wanting to surprise anybody at close range, and we were successful enough that we never saw a bear all day. But, I have never been as aware of their presence as I was that day. Hiking five miles of trail, we passed evidence of countless diggings and saw the tracks of at least four different bears, two blacks and two grizzlies. Coming upon a set of grizzly tracks in the muddy trail my friend bent over for a closer look and abruptly straightened up to scan the slopes in all directions. The tracks were so fresh there was no question that they had been emptied by the bear only moments before. At a moment like that, as much as you'd like to know where the bear is, it hardly matters that you didn't see it.

One of the pleasures and challenges of living in bear country is tuning into the presence of something nearby but not visible, something more aware of you than you are of it. Seeing the bear is a singular opportunity for wonder, but not seeing it shouldn't disappoint you, especially if you've already come to know it through its marks. ////

Bears will strip the bark from trees to reach the sweet cambium layer beneath.

A *black bear will leave the shadows of the forest to fish or drink, but will retreat again to the cool shade and protection of the trees.*

While this coastal grizzly digs for clams, a cautious red fox stands by waiting hopefully for leftovers.

The teddy-look is but a decepive mask to the strength and ferocity of a wild bear.

Bears are nature's great rock rollers–who knows what kind of treats may be hiding underneath?

For most people the sight of a bear print may be as close as they'll ever get to the real thing, and for most people that's close enough.

MOUNTAIN GRIZZLY

I WAS HIKING UP HIGH THAT October day, carrying my shotgun, hoping to jump grouse. When I reached the ridge I looked over into the maw, the velvet green bowl of uncut valley on the other side—the largest roadless area in the valley. It was windy up there, and cold. Just looking at that modest sweep of green, that sanctuary, soothed something inside me, relaxed so many tensions stored up—as when you or someone else places their hands over your face, covering your eyes, and then runs the fingertips slowly down and over your face, drawing out all the worry lines. That's what it felt like, over my heart, and I felt happiness.

If there were any other animals stirring—ravens drifting overhead or ground squirrels scurrying—I don't remember them. I walked south along the ridge, and out of the corner of my eye I noticed footprints in that new snow, fresh human footprints, I thought, and my mind went, *Ah, damn—someone's been up here on snowshoes.* And there was that usual momentary feeling of loss and confusion when, having believed you were alone in the woods, you find out there is another. All the solitary senses are scrambled; you begin to readjust, to redefine the woods. The wildness leaves you like wind leaving a sail.

I started to not even go over and look at the tracks. I started to just turn around and go back down the mountain in the direction I'd come from, to be sure I wouldn't risk seeing that person—but something, I'm not sure what, pulled me over to look at the tracks. It might have had something to do with the size of them.

The majesty of the grizzly bear is equaled only by the majesty of the wild country it inhabits.

And it seemed a bit goofy to me that someone would be way up here on snowshoes when they weren't needed at all—there were just a couple of inches of snow.

I went over to the tracks and stood over them and froze like a scarecrow. They were picture-book grizzly tracks, slab footed, with the long claws, and for a moment—as when you first awaken from a dream—I could not make sense of the size of them. I could tell they were grizzly, but the size of them shut something down in my mind. My little 20-gauge popgun, the little iron stick with the little cardboard shells in it, felt like a crooked twig in my hand. I felt as if I were suddenly filled with straw and existed for no other purpose than to have the stuffing knocked out of me.

The tracks were glistening, the snow crushed and still watery from the heat of the bear's foot. I had moved him out just ahead of me, and by the casualness of the gait, he (?)—there were no cubs' prints—had not been in any kind of hurry.

I don't know how long I stood there. In all my years in the valley, and in all the thousands of miles hiked, I'd seen grizzlies twice, both times at close range, but this, the size of the tracks and the beauty of the location—up on this windy spine, up on my favorite mountain in the valley—moved me in a way I had not been moved before. I stood there and held on to the feeling of fear and joy mixed, almost hypnotized by the strength of the two emotions. I had viewed this as my mountain, up to this point. I knew where the elk bedded down, where the berries were best, where the moose lived, and the grouse, the coyotes.

I had to follow the tracks—had to see where they went, what that bear's habits were—even if only for a short distance.

I wanted to see the bear.

There could be no evolutionary advantage to such a longing. It had to lie in the realm of spillover—the magic, beyond what makes sense to our short-term goals. It had to be in the realm of art. I moved along the ridge carefully, head down, studying—and loving—those tracks.

It's a valley of giants: of herons, bald eagles, golden eagles; white sturgeon below the falls and twenty-five-pound bull trout; lions, wolves, bears, great gray owls, great horned owls, moose, elk—all *big* animals—but seeing this grizzly would be like seeing an elephant in the woods, so alien would it be to see such a giant. Because they're trophy-hunted, because the dominant, wide-ranging, no-fearing ones are selected against, the giant grizzlies—like the country around them—are becoming smaller with each generation.

I moved carefully, slowly, through the lodgepole pines. My body told me to turn around and leave, as did my mind—but there was some other sense, some other thing, that drew me, that overrode those two imperatives. I felt it and trusted it and walked carefully down the trail, being careful not to step in the tracks and feeling very fortunate, very lucky to be on the same mountain with this bear, to be at virtually the same point in time and space as he.

I felt something filling me, coming up from the ground, some kind of juice, some wildness, some elixir. I walked slowly, expecting to see the giant head and shoulders just ahead of me at any second, looking back.

But there was nothing—nothing other than cold air and winter coming. To my right, to the west, lay the beautiful, safe, uncut velvet of the roadless area—the wilderness. To my left, below and beyond me, lay the swaths of clearcuts. This was the edge, and it seemed very much to me that the giant grizzly, more like a cave bear than a present-day grizzly, was walking the edge of his territory, checking it out before he went back into the earth to sleep for five or six months. Checking things out, noting the new roads below and the new savaged hillsides, the patchwork of them leaping ever closer. And I imagined it was some ritual he did every year, and I hoped that his sleep was not as troubled as mine.

There was no trouble in my soul, in my heart that afternoon. There was only glory and wonder—only peace and awe.

The tracks disappeared as the bear walked out of the thin snow, as the new snow disappeared into open patches of sun. I thought of how the mild sun must feel on his thick coat, which might weigh as much as 100 pounds. I thought of the sweeping length of his claws. How can the world still have such a wondrous beast in it—just on the edge of surviving, but still here?

The disappearance of his tracks was good for another shot of reverence, fear, and euphoria. It was like making some small new discovery in your science, when one curious piece of data connects with another. It was like writing a sentence that surprises and pleases you, that both ties into that which has come before and opens a door into new country.

I paused, wanting more. I pushed on in the direction I felt he had gone.

After a little while the wild juice inside me, the fizz of it, waned a bit, and I knew I was off his track. I was still out in open country; he must have swung down into the trees, into the sanctu-ary of cover. I sat down on a cold rock in the wind, tried to feel the sun on my face, and just rested. I sat there for a good long while and thought about what I had seen. There was a feeling as when you are in the presence of a great man or woman, someone who has meant a lot to you in your life and in others' lives, and whom you finally get to meet. You want to savor the moment and say the right thing, but also, especially if the day has been long and that person is tired, you don't want to be a weight. And so you savor the moment and are reassured, almost relieved, to see that, yes, there is something special and different about him or her, some force, something inde-finable—a thing you can see and hear and feel, but not know or name. And then you say good-bye and leave, soon enough to keep from being, lovingly but clumsily, stone weight.

That was how I left the mountain: grateful, more than grateful, for having seen the tracks, and for the bear's having heard me coming and having moved slowly away from me rather than toward me; and feeling that it was very important not to overstay.

I'd seen a bear on this mountain before—a grizzly. I'd seen a little black bear too, had just walked up on him, to within twenty feet of him as he sat there upwind, looking around as if confused. I'd also seen a big grizzly up here about five or six years ago. Not as big as this one; it had been standing on a log looking down at me as I picked berries. My two dogs were with me, and one of them saw the bear, about 100 yards upslope, standing on that log and looking down at us. Fortunately, it was the dog that minds best—Homer, not Ann. I whispered to Homer (whose hackles were raised) to "leave it," to come over to me. And Homer did. Then I called to Ann in a low voice, and she minded because she did not see or smell the bear and because Homer had not yet growled.

I took the dogs by the collar and went back down the hill, believing that at any second the bear was going to charge. At the bottom of the hill, when I dared look back, the bear was gone. . . .

But that grizzly story was not like this one. It was a fine one, but different. I'd had my dogs with me, and I'd left. This time I was alone, and I followed. It may seem foolish, but this was the only time I've ever done that—followed one. It's the only time I've felt the urge to do that, almost like an invitation. I can't explain it: only that it was a true gut feeling.

Now, as I headed down the mountain, I heard an elk bugling in the woods below, not far from the country I'd come up through. It was a wild, autumnal sound, the high fluting of it seeming somehow to be coming from my own bones, like air through a musical instrument, and out my heart. Even as I listened, the bull ended his challenge with a series of deep coughs and grunts. He was very close, below me.

I was thinking about slipping down into those woods and seeing if I could sneak up close enough to get a look at him when I heard the deep coughs and grunts of another bull answering him, moving in on him—or what I thought at first was another bull.

I wondered for a couple of seconds why the second bull wasn't answering with its own high bugle, why it was just coughing and grunting—a much deeper cough than I'd ever heard from an elk before—and then something in me revealed the truth, and I felt my blood drain from my face and upper body as I realized that the giant bear was hunting that giant elk, maybe trying to lure it in for a fight.

It was a sound from more than a million years ago, a sound from the Pleistocene: a sound from the center of the earth. It took my blood to a place my blood had never been before—old memories, old fears.

It wasn't true terror that I felt. I don't know what it was. I didn't panic. But it took no huge leap of logic for me to intuit that if my *blood* was frightened, or even made uncomfortable, then maybe *I* should be too.

I left, went down the hill, staying downwind of the sounds, having already been graced with more than I could ever have asked for, and needing no more. Above me the two giants kept calling, and I wondered how it would turn out, and whether the grizzly was serious about stalking the bull or was only playing, only curious, as I'd been when I first considered trying to sneak up on the bull. . . .

I decided that next day that I would head up to a big patch of country to the north of me that had not had roads built through it, though it was bordered and ringed by them. I parked along one of those gravel roads and started up into the woods. The sun was orange, over Buckhorn Ridge. I was working along a deer trail, noting old elk sign. It was a shelf along the mountain, a southern exposure, with aspens above and below. I was going to cross it and then go into some big cedars and follow those woods up the mountain a little farther before turning back and heading home. It was the time of day, late in the afternoon, when you are most likely to see all sorts of animals, though because of the strong wind I did not think I would see any. Sometimes the wind was in my face, but other times it quartered from upslope, from the north. The aspen leaves were beautiful, shading to bright yellow, and they rattled in that strong wind.

I came around a bend in the meadow's deer trail—the whole valley below me—and saw a golden bear walking slowly toward me, not forty yards away. Too close; too damn close. She was smallish—about twice my size—and her thick forelegs were chocolate brown, while all the rest of her was sun-struck blond.

The wide face, the round ears, the hump over her shoulder—another grizzly, coming toward me, unlike yesterday's, but averting her gaze, not making eye contact. Swinging her head and shoulders left and right of me, looking everywhere but *at* me. I was stupid enough to believe for a second that she did not know I was there. The wind ruffled her fur, came from behind me now, like a traitor, and in that cold instant I knew that she knew.

Now a yearling cub came behind her, ten or fifteen yards back, looking exceedingly nervous, and then directly behind that one came its twin, also looking troubled: not playing, as cubs do, but looking hesitant, looking uncertain.

We were all too damn close. The mother stopped about thirty yards away—again, my shotgun like a popgun, the villainous wind gusting at my back now—and she turned a quarter turn and pretended to gaze out at the valley below. She was so beautiful, in that disappearing sunlight. It seemed to paint her.

Her cubs came anxiously down the trail behind her—almost dancing in their nervousness, seeming to want to rise on their hind feet and turn away and go back in the other direction, but obliged to follow her—and I understood now that she too was nervous, that she was trying to move me out of her territory.

Instinctively, I turned a quarter turn to the south and look-ed out at the valley too. I dropped my head to show her I was not a threat. I felt fear, but even stronger, apology, even dismay. I felt incredible respect for her too, and a surge of gratitude. We both studied the valley for a moment. I was waiting to see if she would charge—and a thing passed between us, as if we were wired together for a moment: the knowledge and understanding by both of us that she had every right, more than every right, to charge me (whether in bluff or attack, no matter; she was almost *mandated* to charge), and yet she chose not to.

I am convinced it was a conscious decision not to—that it was a thought, a rational decision, the mind overriding the body. It was merciful and generous.

Perhaps only a couple of hundred grizzlies exist in the continental United States outside national parks, and here were three of them, waiting for me to move aside so they could continue down the trail, into history—into whatever fate awaited them.

I turned around and walked away. I walked weak legged down the mountain in blue dusk, the sun now sending up orange sundial rays from its nest for the night, behind the far mountain. I reached the truck in darkness half an hour later and drove home to my wife and daughter. I held on to that new, fresh feeling of still being alive for as long as I could; and I can still feel, can still remember, the gratitude. ////

Subadult bears must remain continually alert to the moods and needs of all the bigger bears in the neighborhood.

Bears will pant like their common ancestors, dogs, to help cool themselves.

The bear with the best concentration has the greatest chance of success.

Bears, like people, are plantigrades—they walk flat-footed.

Following pages: **A** big bear can be surprisingly well camouflaged and difficult to distinguish in heavy cover even at close range.

AN ORIGINAL ESSAY BY
GRETEL EHRLICH

NEIGHBORHOOD BEARS

I'VE SPENT A GOOD MANY years hoping to stumble upon bears rather than avoiding encounters. Maybe it's because I was born in California whose state animal is the grizzly bear, though they were exterminated there long ago. I do believe in some essential equality of all sentient beings. I'm only one of the coinhabitants here and I want to meet my neighbors.

My ranch sat below a cirque of high mountains. Above me were black bears, mountain lions, golden and bald eagles, marmots, voles, pikas, and the summer feeding grounds for elk and deer. But it is the bears that held my a particular interest because I knew they were watching me and that if I tried hard enough, I could see them too.

The first flesh and blood bear I met face-to-face was not a grizzly but a black bear and, admittedly, the meeting startled me. It was the first summer I had lived in Wyoming, and I was herding sheep for a few days to fill in for a sick herder. Sheepcamp was on top of the Big Horn Mountains on a nine-thousand-foot ridge. I lived in a traditional round-topped wagon with a bed built across the back, a tiny wood cookstove and dutch doors that opened out onto thousands of acres of open range, and it was there that my nightly visitor came. It was a young black bear who had fallen in love with my mare.

One August night I fastened my horse to a picket line, fed, grained, and watered her, cooked myself the usual dinner of mutton burger, rice, and beans, and

A *black bear, while smaller than the grizzly or brown bear, is still a formidable animal.*

crawled into my shiptight bed after the sheep had settled down. The night was clear and cold, and the aurora began to throw its white floodlights up into the northern sky. I heard my horse squealing and I threw open the dutch doors to see a bear standing behind the horse, swatting at her rump. I did what a frontier woman usually does—I grabbed a long-handled spoon and a black iron frying pan and beat the hell out of it, making such a racket that the young bear ran away.

But that wasn't the only time a bear paid visits to my camp. After my stint of sheepherding, I lived for the rest of the summer at sheep headquarters—a large log cabin at the edge of a mountaintop meadow surrounded by lodgepole pines. John Hopkin, one of the family owners of the ranch, was foreman of the sheep operation and even though bears preyed on lambs, he liked them. He considered them neighbors. Every day John set a bowl of honey on a log in front of the cabin and every evening at dusk, the same bear licked the bowl clean.

"Look at how neat she is. She cleans the bowl and puts it back on the log where she found it. I wish you were that way," John liked to say, eyeing my messy pile of books, papers, and cameras.

In John's estimation, bears are sometimes better behaved than humans. And perhaps he is right. All I saw in human society was meanness, greed, and destitution, a poverty of spirit that provoked a poverty of means, and I longed for the time before humans were thought to be the dominant creatures of the earth. But it's never felt that way to me out here in bear country. I've developed the habit of getting to know the neighborhoods surrounding me, as I did when living in big cities. And now instead of exploring First Avenue and the Thirties in New York, I try to find where elk and deer have bedded down, where eagles nest, and where the rattlesnake and coyote den. Not that I want to intrude on their lives, I simply want to cohabit the area with them.

One year after reading Frank Craighead's astounding and heartbreaking classic, *Track of the Grizzly*, I tried to find a black bear's den site above my ranch. It was October and I'd moved to a hunting camp perched between a pink granite outcrop and a long meadow jumping with pikas and voles and fed by a spring whose stream was only eight inches wide but whose water was sweeter than any I'd tasted before. Every day I'd ride out from camp on Blue, my old sheepherder horse, and we'd look for bear tracks in fresh snow. I knew some of the neighborhoods of denning bears, how their tracks led from water to gooseberries, to an area of downfallen timber where a den could be excavated under a log. But bears are clever about hiding their whereabouts. I had to be patient and unobtrusive.

Blue and I stayed downwind of the main trail, the downfall, the water source, and the berry bushes. We milled around in a thicket of young trees and I lay on a log while Blue grazed and waited. You can smell a bear before you see one. It's a sour smell—"like the damned mash we used to use to make alcohol in the stills up here," one old sheepherder used to say. And the crashing noise they make walking through the timber is unlike any other forest noise. In the near primordial silence of those mountains, a bear walking can sound like a Mack truck that took a wrong turn.

One afternoon I finally saw her. She was a young bear, and not wily enough to have noticed me. As she ambled along the main trail the fat and black fur on her back rolled and glistened in autumn sun. When she heard the horse shifting his weight, she stopped, stood up, pointed her nose in the air first one way, then another, and deciding there was no danger, dropped down on all fours, and walked into the woods.

I went back to camp but later that afternoon I returned and followed her tracks a little closer. From a distance I saw the den. It was on a slight rise overlooking a steep canyon, and hidden under brush, a hole had been dug in under a massive fallen log. I took my bearings so I wouldn't forget where it was, and then left, planning to explore the den when I knew she wouldn't be there.

That day didn't come until March. Bears are only partial hibernators and when the chinook winds came down from Alberta in the spring, they brought a few days of bright sunshine and heat. It was on one of those brilliant March days that I returned to the den and sure enough, saw that the bear had left her den. Her tracks indicated she had traveled through the deep snow to water, to where she had turned over logs looking for grubs, and where she had picked over the remains of frozen rose hips. It was then that I decided it was safe enough to crawl into her den to take a look. Inside the den the sour stench was strong but the interior was, in bear architecture terms, lovely.

Bears are tidy housekeepers. There was a narrow entry-way, then a hollowed-out room with a sleeping platform constructed of pine tree boughs laid down together. The huge log spanning the ceiling was a structural beam, big enough to support a cathedral. Though the ground was frozen, the den was warm inside, sheltered from wind coming off drifting snow. On the floor where the bear had lain during the cold months, the ground was packed down flat and beside the sleeping platform was a single pinecone, as if that had been the bear's one toy.

I looked around quickly, put my nose to the walls and floors of the den, touched the log rafter above my head, then made my escape, backing out of the den, and walking in a huge loop upwind from the bear before I dropped down to the steep trail home.

Bears are marvelous architects, but it's their sociability, adaptiveness, and omnivorousness that I think of when I'm around them—not their opportunistic and combative traits. With a bear, as with a human, there is latitude, there is the possibility of compromise. The first people who lived on the central California coast, where I live now, considered the bear the most powerful being around and at big celebrations the bear song was sung by a dancer who sported bear paws around his neck and carried a rattle made of turtle shells filled with small stones. Perhaps it is because we recognize ourselves in bears that we feel connected to them, our shared traits bind us. They can be sleepy, lazy, cranky, curious, cuddly, smart, violent, or bored. They like to travel widely and to keep their young near. And when the first snow falls, they travel hundreds of miles across mountain ranges and rivers to get back to their denning site, waiting for a heavy snowfall so their tracks will fill up as fast as they make them. Then, as winter comes on hard, they disappear. ////

The animal we call a black bear may actually be any of a variety of colors from jet black to blond.

Black bears feed mainly on vegetation, but they do fish and are good at it.

A *black bear will stake out a prime berry bush and strip it clean.*

Bears have few enemies and they rarely lose a fight, except to a larger bear.

Given no choice, black bears are willing to remain very close together along salmon streams.

Black bears of all ages are adept climbers, whereas grizzly bears rarely climb trees.

TÔRNÂRSSUK

THE SEASCAPE WAS ALMOST without color beneath a low gray sky. Scattered ice floes damped any motion of large waves, and fogs and thin snow showers came and went in the still air. The surface of the water was the lacquered black of Japanese wooden boxes.

Three of us stood in the small open boat, about a hundred miles off the northwest coast of Alaska, at the southern edge of the polar pack in the Chukchi Sea. I and two marine scientists were hunting ringed seals that cold September day. In the seal stomachs we found what fish they had been eating; from bottom trawls we learned what the fish they were eating had eaten; and from plankton samplings we learned what the creatures the fish ate were eating.*

We had been working at this study of marine food chains for several weeks, moving west in our boat across the north coast of Alaska, from the west end of the Jones Islands to Point Barrow. At Barrow we boarded a 300-foot oceanographic research vessel, the *Oceanographer*, and headed out into the Chukchi Sea. Each morning for the next two weeks our boat was lowered from the deck of this mother vessel and we worked in the sea ice until evening.

We had been hunting seals intensively for three days without success. Twice we had seen a seal, each time for only a split second. We moved slowly, steadily, through the ice floes, without conversation, occasionally raising a pair of field glasses to study a small, dark dot

*This project was part of a Bureau of Land Management/Outer Continental Shelf study of Alaskan coastal marine life, results of which were to lead offshore oil development in the least harmful direction.

The polar bear is not just a white grizzly. Its sleek and streamlined shape has evolved and adapted to life in the Arctic.

on the water—a piece of ice? A bird? A seal breaking the surface of the water to breathe? It is not so difficult to learn to distinguish among these things, to match a "search image" in the mind after a few days of tutoring with the shading, shape, and movement that mean *seal*. Waiting in silence, intently attentive, was harder to learn.

We were three good sets of eyes, hunting hard. Nothing. A fog would clear. A snow squall drift through. In the most promising areas of the ice we shut off the engines and drifted with the currents. The ice, despite its occasional vertical relief, only compounded a sense of emptiness in the landscape, a feeling of directionlessness. The floes were like random, silent pieces of the earth. Our compass, turning serenely in its liquid dome, promised, if called upon to do so, to render points on a horizon obliterated in slanting snow and fog.

We drifted and sipped hot liquids, and stared into the quiltwork of gray-white ice and ink-black water. If one of us tensed, the others felt it and were alert. Always we were *hunting*. This particular habitat, the number of cod in the water, the time of the year—everything said ringed seals should be here. But for us they weren't.

Late summer in the sea ice. Eventually the cold, damp air finds its way through insulated boots and wool clothing to your bones. The conscious mind, the mind that knows how long you have been out here, importunes for some measure of comfort. We made a slow, wide turn in the boat, a turn that meant the end of the day. Though we still watched intently, thoughts of the ship were now upon us. Before this, we had camped on the beach in

tents; now a hot shower, an evening meal in light clothing at a table, and a way to dry clothes awaited us. In the back of your mind at the end of the day you are very glad for these things.

My friend Bob saw the bear first: an ivory-white head gliding in glassy black water 300 feet ahead, at the apex of a V-wake. We slowed the boat and drew up cautiously to within thirty feet. A male. The great seal hunter himself. About three years old, said Bob.

The bear turned in the water and regarded us with irritation, and then, wary, he veered toward a floe. In a single motion of graceful power he rose from the water to the ice, his back feet catching the ice edge at the end of the movement. Then he stepped forward and shook. Seawater whirled off in flat sheets and a halo of spray. His head lowered, he glared at us with small, dark eyes. Then he crossed the floe and, going down on his forelegs, sliding headfirst, he entered the water on the other side without a splash and swam off.

We found our way to him again through the ice. We were magnetically drawn, in a fundamental but perhaps callow way. Our presence was interference. We approached as slowly as before, and he turned to glower, treading water, opening his mouth—the gray tongue, the pale violet mouth, the white teeth—to hiss. He paddled away abruptly to a large floe and again catapulted from the water, shook his fur out, and started across the ice to open water on the far side.

We let him go. We watched him, that undeterred walk of authority. "The farmer," the whalers had called him, for his "very agricultural appearance as he stalks leisurely over the furrowed fields of ice." John Muir, on a visit to these same waters in 1899, said bears move "as if the country had belonged to them always."

The polar bear is a creature of Arctic edges: he hunts the ice margins, the surface of the water, and the continental shore. The ice bear, he is called. His world forms beneath him in the days of shortening light, and then falls away in the spring. He dives to the ocean floor for mussels and kelp, and soundlessly breaks the water's glassy surface on his return, to study a sleeping seal. Twenty miles from shore he treads water amid schooling fish. The sea bear. In winter, while the grizzly hibernates, the polar bear is out on the sea ice, hunting. In summer his tracks turn up a hundred miles inland, where he has feasted on crowberries and blueberries.

Until a few years ago this resourceful hunter was in a genus by himself: *Thalarctos.* Now he is back where he started, with the grizzly and black bear in the genus *Ursus,* where his genes, if not his behavior, say he belongs.

What was so impressive about the bear we saw that day in the Chukchi was how robust he seemed. At three years of age a bear in this part of the Arctic is likely spending its first summer alone. To feed itself, it has had to learn to hunt, and open pack ice is among the toughest of environments for bears to hunt in. This was September, when most bears are thin, waiting for the formation of sea ice, their hunting platform. In our three days of diligent searching, in this gray and almost featureless landscape of ice remnants so far off the coast, we had seen but two seals. We were transfixed by the young bear. We watched him move off across the ice, into a confusing plane of grays and whites. We were shivering a little and opened a thermos of coffee. A snow shower moved quickly through, and when it cleared we could barely make him out in the black water with field glasses from the rocking boat. A young and successful hunter, at home in his home.

He had found the seals. ////

Polar bears travel vast distances over Arctic regions to find their prey.

A mother bear will use her great body to shelter her young against the Arctic wind.

The polar bear is an expert in the field of deep and total relaxation.

Every minute of the day holds a potential lesson for a bear cub learning to mimic its mother's behavior.

AN ORIGINAL ESSAY BY

JEREMY SCHMIDT

SPRING TRACKS

WINTER ON THE YELLOWSTONE Plateau is a long but clearly defined season. It begins in October with the first permanent snow, and it ends in April with grizzlies. As quickly as that: the season turns on a track in the mud.

I lived at Old Faithful for several years in the 1970s, when snowmobiles were rare and winters were quiet. Time moved slowly, or so it seemed. I could watch the seasons pass at their leisurely pace—especially winter, which became downright obstinate by March. It didn't matter how much a person loved winter; there came a time when everyone was ready for a change.

In my first year, I learned how fast that change could come. March had departed according to its astronomical schedule, but winter stayed on like an unwanted guest. Snow still lay deep over the high country, old snow forming a crust on top of a whole winter's worth of accumulation—six to eight feet of it lying layered and full of a season's history. But then the day came, as it does every spring, when warm winds from the southwest arrived, bringing with them the intoxicating odor of thawing earth. Up from the lowlands, up from the awakening soil of Idaho wheat fields, it was the smell of things growing, moving—a restless smell that made me want to walk, not ski. So I pulled on rubber-bottomed boots and went out to the geyser basin.

The thermally warmed ground was free of snow. It felt good to have my feet on something solid. The sun was so warm it felt hot. The warmth made me lazy, and I walked slowly.

About a mile from the house, I came across the

The grizzly bear was named for the grizzled appearance of its coat with various combinations of lighter and darker hairs.

bones of a winter-killed bison. No surprise: I had watched him die back in February. He had moved into a small clearing around a hot spring, and in his last days stood motionless, too weak to push aside the deep snow, too weak to reach the frozen grass below. He became weaker because of his weakness—riding a steady and solitary spiral into death. He grew so thin that I could see his ribs and pelvis through the heavy shag of his winter coat. Finally he lay down and did not get up, and two days later he was dead. The ravens took his eyes first. The coyotes took his bowels, then the rest of him. They turned him into winter music, their choruses echoing across the snowy hills.

Now his bones, picked clean and bleached white like old snow, lay scattered over the steaming ground. I picked up the pelvis, and was surprised by its light weight. Beside it I found a femur, stout with a bulbous end like a club. Not a bad weapon, I thought, lazily thumping it into my palm, and (as if the thoughts were related), not a bad way to die either—I mean, to lie down on warm ground, alone with whatever thoughts come at the end of a bison's life, and to slip away leaving behind only white and beautiful bones.

Death and springtime. Bones in the season of rebirth. These are not contradictions, nor are they opposites. In death there is life, and in all life lie the seeds of death. Together they are an expression of continuity. For me on that warm spring day, these were peaceful thoughts. Had the ground not been damp sulphur-smelling clay, I might have stretched out for a nap.

Instead, I kept poking among the bones, and it was there, where the rib cage lay on a blanket of matted bison fur, that I got my lesson in how winter ends. Grizzly tracks! Big, well-defined footpads, claw tips pushed deep into the mud. In one place his forefoot had slid on the slick surface; the claws had raked deep grooves. I took him to be a male because they were the tracks of an adult, and an adult female in April would most likely be trailed by a cub or two. This was a single bear. He had rolled the rib cage, found nothing here to eat, and gone on. He had gone, but in passing he had taken a firm hold on my mind. Suddenly the day came alive. I was wide awake, listening, watching. A grizzly was out, and that changed everything. After a winter of no bears, of bears being asleep, they were back. The appearance of this one cleaved winter from the rest of the year as sharply as if it had been dropped on a razor.

I didn't see the him that day. I didn't need to see him. Just knowing he was in the neighborhood changed the atmosphere in a palpable way. More than any other wild animal in North America, grizzlies have the power to alter a landscape through the simple fact of their presence.

Aldo Leopold understood this. In his classic book, *A Sand County Almanac,* he describes a mountain in New Mexico called Escudilla, a distinctive landmark visible for miles around, and home to a solitary grizzly bear.

No one ever saw the old bear, but in the muddy springs about the base of the cliffs you saw his incredible tracks. Seeing them made the most hard-bitten cowboys aware of bear. Wherever they rode they saw the mountain, and when they saw the mountain they thought of bear. Campfire conversation ran to beef, bailes, and bear. He was the only surviving grizzly in the region. He had no chance of reproducing. He could have died a natural death, and you might think that even his enemies would have allowed him that, as a sort of gesture to the last of his kind. Instead, he was hunted down by a government trapper sent to kill predators. In death, the Escudilla grizzly bore no resemblance to the powerful presence he had exerted when alive. He had become a mere carcass, not even the pelt worth saving. Seeing this had a big effect on Leopold, who was working for the Forest Service at the time. He wrote that only after the grizzly had been killed did he and other rangers begin to consider the loss. Recalling the conquistador Coronado:

We spoke harshly of the Spaniards who, in their zeal for gold and converts, had needlessly extinguished the native Indians. It did not occur to us that we, too, were the captains of an invasion too sure of its own righteousness.

Escudilla still hangs on the horizon, but when you see it you no longer think of bear. It's only a mountain now. The West is covered with empty mountains. Grizzlies walk a shrinking range. We have driven them out, and replaced their great spirits with nothing. Their former homelands, even those whose scenery we have preserved, have been emptied. Once highly visible on the plains (Lewis and Clark reported numerous, often dramatic encounters), grizzly bears have become shy denizens of a few protected high-altitude sanctuaries. In the Lower Forty-eight states, only the wildlands around Yellowstone and Glacier national parks still provide for grizzlies.

Typically, you don't see them. They are like the Lord of Escudilla—on the edge of vision but central to awareness. Speaking for myself, I like having them there. I like thinking about them, and knowing that they are out there. I'm not sure I want them closer. In fact I'm pretty sure I don't. Every encounter I've had with a bear reinforces that feeling.

One summer night I camped on a sand spit along the shore of an alpine lake. It was a bright night, the moon nearly full. I fell asleep on my back with the tent door open, and awoke some time later to a darkness in the tent doorway. Opening my extremely nearsighted eyes, I made out a black shape hovering above me. Actually I think it was the terrible smell that woke me. Bears are renowned for having keen noses, but I have to wonder how a bear can smell anything when the bear itself smells so bad. I fought the urge to shrink toward the back of the tent, to turn over and sit up. If you encounter a bear, all the experts tell us, don't move. Sure as hell don't run or struggle. So there I lay, inhaling the stink, until the darkness moved away. When I got the nerve to put on my glasses and slide out the tent door for a look, there was nothing to see except bare sand and the moonlit lake.

The bear had come and gone like a malodorous dream. An apparition? No. In the morning I found tracks of more than one bear on that strip of sand, and thinking it over, I realized that I had put my tent square on a natural travel route. I might as well have put it in the middle of a road.

That experience changed my methods of choosing campsites in bear country. It's not important where you want to sleep; better to find a spot well away from ursine traffic. This works well to avoid nighttime bear visits, but what about the Escudilla kind?

Those dominant spirits? They live in your brain, and there's not much you can do to get away from them.

I had walked alone into the northern end of the Teton Range in late October, eager to make one last overnight trip before winter. Evening found me in an area of mixed meadow and open forest about three miles from the trailhead: good bear country, and the sort of place that encourages a hiker to take precautions. Looking around for a campsite, I chose what seemed to be a perfect spot—an open, gravel-covered knob about an acre in extent surrounded by willow bushes and a few small trees. It was on the way to nowhere else, and several hundred yards from the nearest trail.

After dark, I lay my bag out under a clear sky and climbed in. The flush of warmth mingled with delicious tiredness. I watched the stars for a while, expecting to drift peacefully into sleep, but sleep would not come. I couldn't get the image of grizzly bears out of my mind.

But why? I ran through a mental checklist of rules for camping in bear country. There was no sign of recent bear activity. I had not cooked supper near my sleeping site; in fact I hadn't cooked supper at all. Anything having to do with food was 200 yards away in my pack, downwind, hung high from a tree. I kept sitting up and looking around, shining my flashlight in a slow circle. No eyes glowed out there in the dark. No sound broke the frosty silence. Lying down again, I told myself there was no reason to be nervous.

Nothing helped. After an hour of wakefulness, I got up and spread all my loose gear in a big circle around my sleeping bag, a sort of warning circle to stake out my territory and tell a bear that I was there. As a final gesture, I went around the circle again, scent-marking, coyote-style, pissing on bushes and stones. In hundreds of nights camping in bear country, I had never done anything like that. I had never felt the need. My actions were spontaneous. I was improvising, trying to say, "This place is mine!"

Still I couldn't sleep. Repeatedly, my pulse hammered me awake until in the end, feeling foolish but with no doubts about what I had to do, I gathered my things, crammed them into my pack, and walked out of there, back to the trailhead, flashing my light in all directions. The trail was dry and frozen most of the way, except in a few low areas where the soft mud was just starting to harden. I looked for bear tracks; there were none. Yet in the morning, as I sat on the tailgate of my pickup brewing coffee, wishing I hadn't spooked out of my camp like a worried chicken, a man on horseback came up the trail. An elk hunter, he'd been out since before dawn. "Morning," he said, and yes he'd be happy for a cup of coffee. Had he seen any elk? I asked. No, but back a couple of miles, near where the forest broke into meadows, there were some fine fresh bear tracks in the mud. Coming this way.

So. There was a bear, and it had walked the trail behind me. But what did that mean? This was grizzly country after all; I should expect to see some sign. A few tracks didn't give me reason to feel I had been at risk. They didn't give me a good excuse for walking out of the wilderness in the dark.

I still wonder about the urgency I felt that night. I am tempted to believe that I sensed the bear's presence, and something about its aura warned of danger. But if that were the case, I mean if I had some sixth-sense ability to perceive bears, I would expect it to help me in other situations.

The time I thought a grizzly bear was a moose, it failed me completely. I wasn't asleep or dreaming or dizzy. I was wide awake, walking a game trail south of the Tetons. I had never seen a bear in that area. I thought it was too far south for grizzlies. Some distance down the hill I had seen bear tracks but they were indistinct, and I assumed them to be made by a black bear. Not that black bears are to be dismissed, but they don't pack the psychic wallop of a grizzly. My mind was on elk and moose, whose recent tracks filled the trail.

A cold autumn rain had fallen earlier in the day, softening the ground so I could walk in complete silence. I was coming around the brow of a hill, climbing gently. There was no wind, but a soft downhill airflow was in my face. It brought to my ears the sound of a large animal breaking branches, the sort of noise a bull moose makes when beating up vegetation with his antlers. There were no trees on the slope—just meadow grass—but I knew there was a wooded draw out of sight below the crest, and I assumed that if I moved silently, I would be able to look into the draw and see the moose without his knowing I was there.

Each step took me a few inches higher. I moved very slowly. The tops of the trees came into view, then the lower branches. The snapping and breaking continued. I stared hard, my attention firmly on the draw 200 feet away.

What happened next was like a movie when the camera suddenly changes focus and you realize that a fuzzy shape in the foreground is actually something worth looking at. Without moving, my eyes shifted their focus from the trees to the grass, from 200 feet to twelve. At the same moment, my brain made a couple of quick jumps. That tussock was not grass; it was tawny fur. I wasn't hearing branches being broken, it was grass stems and tiny twigs. It wasn't a moose, it was a grizzly. With its head down, digging for roots, the bear hadn't seen me yet, which gave me a chance, if I backed away quietly enough, to avoid creating a disturbance. Lucky for me, I was able to do that.

From my perspective, the story is like Escudilla in reverse. A place I once considered empty of grizzlies is not empty. It is no longer just a mountain. Whenever I walk in that area I will think about bears. I will look for their tracks in the spring. I will watch for signs of their presence. I will hope to keep them on the edge of my vision, and in the center of my awareness. ////

Following pages: **T**ypically an adult sow grizzly bear has a litter of two cubs every three years. With such a low reproductive rate, bear populations are easily overharvested.

One way to distingush a grizzly bear from a black bear is the grizzly's "dished-in" profile.

Deep snow is little deterrent to the strength of a mature bear.

EXCERPTED FROM *NO ROOM FOR BEARS* BY

FRANK DUFRESNE

THE TWENTY-FIFTH BEAR

EVER SINCE THE APPEARANCE of their ancestors on earth, man and bears have been at odds. Beginning in the Pleistocene when giant cave bears towered over every other predator—of which man must be reckoned as one—our low-browed grandfathers were forced to cope with shaggy-haired beasts who stood twice as tall and outweighed them ten to one. For half a million years it was the bear, not man, who dominated the wilds, and it continued to hold the upper edge until the development of high-powered rifles within the past 200 years.

In this short period—the blink of an eye in time—some of the bears have not adjusted their thinking to man's sudden supremacy. Some of them still believe they can whip any man in a fair fight, and that they have every right to run him out of the dwindling wilderness. My friend, Hosea, the greatest bear student I ever knew, used to say that about one grizzly out of twenty-five is ready to do battle against a human for reasons best known to themselves. "Unfortunately," Hosea would add slyly, "they don't wear numbers on their backs like football players so you never can be sure when you've met the twenty-fifth bear."

I knew what he meant, because I had searched unsuccessfully for one of these "twenty-fifth" bears. It had all started when a forest ranger was mauled to death by a grizzly while cruising timber on Admiralty Island. His death was to start another public outcry to remove all protection on Alaskan bears, put a bounty on the killers, poison them, get rid of them all. Of the several fatal attacks and maimings of humans by grizzlies, the

*T*hrough their posturing and threatening behavior, bears often are able to settle arguments short of violence.

case of the forest ranger was to create the most attention.

But, of course, the ranger would never know about this furor. All he knew was that a bear lurked nearby in the rain forest and that he would take no chances with it. The minute he laid eyes on it he would drop it in its tracks. He couldn't afford to be careless. It was too dark; the bear would be too close. So the ranger had made up his mind to shoot quickly if the animal showed the first sign of a fight.

Evidence of its nearness was clear to a woodsman of the forest ranger's experience. There was the much used wallow hole filled with still roily water, and the huge padded prints in the soft mud alongside. A spruce tree near the game trail down which the ranger and his unarmed helper were traveling had been shredded of its bark as high as he could reach with the muzzle of his rifle. Matted brown hair clung to the oozing pitch. In the trail itself was the real payoff—a half-eaten salmon fresh out of the creek.

The ranger held up his hand in silent, tense warning to his young aid, who was following close with a bulky packload of camp supplies. The rifle came out of the crook of his left arm; his right index finger slid inside the trigger guard, and his thumb pressed hard against the safety lever. This might have to be quick.

He listened carefully. There was no sound except that of their own heavy breathing and the flop-flop of spawning coho salmon in the small stream that ran around the bottom of the knoll on which they stood. Both men were dead sure now that the bear was near; that it must have sensed them and had chosen to stand its ground. You get to feel things like this when your job is scouting timber on the primitive forest lands of Admiralty Island with its

estimated population of 1,600 bears!

Later, when I talked with the young backpacker, he told me he saw the grizzly first, and hissed an excited warning to the ranger. Silent as a shadow, the bear had risen off its bed between three closely growing hemlocks and faced them with lowered head. The distance was twenty feet. For a half minute the small eyes stared at them. The helper said he would never forget; they were like two red marbles. He saw the black, rubbery lips separate to bare yellowed teeth.

At the crash of the rifle the young backpacker told me he jumped off the knoll and went rolling and clawing down through prickly devil's-club to the creek bottom. Wrestling out of his pack, he scrambled to a smallish tree and swarmed up until he reached a point level with the knoll-top. The ranger was not in sight. The bear was bouncing about insanely with movements so fast it was all a blur to the helper's eyes. When the beast backed away for a second he saw the ranger face down on the ground trying to push himself up with his arms. The helper got one horrified glimpse of clothing ripped to rags, of bloody, gaping wounds. Then the bear rushed in again, roaring and mauling and shaking the man until he was limp.

The helper said he didn't recall too clearly what then happened. At the sight of his partner's stricken body, he dropped to the ground and climbed up the knoll hoping in some vague way to recover the rifle and get in a telling shot with it. But when he reached the ranger he knew it was too late. The bear had vented its rage and fled the scene. There was nothing to do except try to bandage the awful wounds, build a campfire, and keep a death watch through the ensuing night.

He had trouble locating the rifle. A blow of the bear's paw had spun it from the ranger's hands and sent it flying far into the brush. It had been fired once, the empty brass case ejected, and a fresh cartridge fed halfway into the firing chamber. Here was mute testimony of the terrific speed of the charge, because the ranger had been fairly adept in the handling of firearms. He must have had less than a second from the time he fired the first hurried shot until the beast struck him down.

When the young helper showed me the spot a few days later it was our hope to destroy the bear before it attacked another human. An Indian tracker picked up the footprints and we followed them into the high meadows above timberline before they faded out. There was no sign of blood. A year elapsed before Hosea came to see me with what he said was a hunch. He reasoned that if the bear had not been wounded too severely, with the passage of time it might return to its old fishing hole.

It was a rainy, gloomy day on the sixteenth of October—a year to the day since the attack— when Hosea left his gas boat at the mouth of the river. Before rowing ashore in a small skiff, he instructed his boating companion to wait aboard until noon of the next day before attempting to follow his trail up the river. "I was up against a wily, dangerous grizzly," said the guide later. "Having once been stung by a rifle bullet and having killed the man who fired the shot, that bear would have a savage reception ready for the next human to invade its domain." But Hosea had confidence in his own ability and told his shipmate to listen for shooting late in the afternoon. If there had been a successful encounter he would fire three fast shots.

In the lower stretches of the river Hosea saw almost no sign of bear that day. The early runs of humpback and dog salmon were over and the carcasses of spawned-out fish had been washed into the bay by heavy fall rains. But up in the narrow headwaters Hosea knew that the late spawning cohos would still be threshing out their redds in the gravel, and that each favorite site would have its quota of bears. He saw two yearlings searching the empty riffles ahead, and waited until they went into the timber before proceeding. He had no intention of letting them squall an alarm to the bears upstream.

At noon the guide reached the forks where the particular stream he was seeking joined the main river. There had been dozens of small tributaries, but Hosea was too good a woodsman to stray off the penciled directions I—as director of the Game Commission—had made for him. As he told me later, he found part of a rusted kerosene lantern abandoned by the litter-bearing party the year before, and noted places where the blueberry bushes had been axed away to let the carriers through with their lifeless burden. As he neared the scene of the killing, Hosea said, he became extremely cautious, stopping to test the wind and sometimes standing motionless for minutes at a time. It was a spooky sort of place under the canopy of giant trees, fog-shrouded and dim. Few men would care to venture alone here to match wits with one of the wiliest and most savage of all wild game.

The distance was now less than a quarter of a mile to the knoll. Hosea deliberately waited for the late afternoon hours in the hope of catching the bear out in the stream where he could spy it first. When he could see the pool, there were parts of salmon on the bank where a bear had eaten its fill. Was it the same bear? As Hosea eased lightly past the deep imprints of a grizzly, its fetid odor hung heavy in the dank air, and he knew he was very close. In spite of his long experience among these bears, Hosea admitted to a prickly feeling along his scalp. "I could feel death all around me," he confessed.

At the foot of a leaning windfall where a giant hemlock had been uprooted by a windstorm and crashed into the forks of another tree, Hosea stopped to recheck his rifle again. He was carrying his favorite .30-06 sporter, equipped now with receiver sight with open aperture for fast shooting. The cartridges were well-tested 220-grain open point, expanding—deadly if they struck a vital spot. Hosea had heard that the forest ranger had trusted his life to regular Army issue hardpoints, filed square for dumdum effect. The guide had no faith in such makeshift ammunition. Removing first one hand and then the other from the damp gunstock, he wiped them dry against the wool shirt under his light slicker-jacket. His eyes measured the trunk of the windfall, selecting steps among the exposed roots where he could mount in a hurry if need be.

"I'd come far enough," said Hosea. "I'd gambled on the grizzly being at this spot. But now all I heard were cohos in the creek and the drip-drip of rain."

Call it premonition, sixth sense, or what you will, Hosea, who was not in the habit of loading the chamber of his rifle until he was ready to fire, now drew back the bolt and eased a cartridge into firing position. The operation was barely audible—a light, oily *snick*. But it triggered an explosive roar, followed by a crescendo of trumpet-blasts that reverberated through the forest. The spine-

chilling outbursts seemed to come from everywhere. The instant he heard them Hosea mounted quickly to the windfall and ran upward until he stood on the leaning trunk fifteen feet above a dense patch of devil's-club. He knew now that the beast had been watching for him. With the hateful scent of man full in its nostrils it had been silently closing in for the attack at the very second Hosea's hunch had caused him to work the bolt of his rifle. Hosea thinks the grizzly still remembered the slight, metallic click that had preceded a rifle blast on another October day.

In its baffled fury the bear thrashed about in the heavy cover trying to flush out the man enemy. By climbing to a point overhead, Hosea had suddenly cut off his fresh scent. Air currents with their tendency to swirl upward were all at once lost to the bear. Looking down on the crazed beast now, there was no longer any doubt in Hosea's mind that this was the grizzly that had taken a man's life. In all his years of working among the bears of southeastern Alaska he had never witnessed such rage; had never seen a bear so determined to attack. Unable to see its foe, its roars and rapidly ejaculated *chuff-chuff-chuff* of clashing teeth changed to whining eagerness.

Midway in its crashing leaps the bear suddenly froze motionless. A vagrant down-scent had carried Hosea's location to its nose. It rose on hind feet and for ten long seconds looked upward to study the face of the enemy. Hosea's shot was cool, unhurried, and accurate. There was no need for a second cartridge. Watching the slumped carcass to make certain it was all over, Hosea retraced his steps to the ground and moved forward to prod the bear in the back of its neck with the toe of his boot. Gripping one of the big, furry ears he swung the bulky head around to look for wounds. Down near the shoulder was a long, healed scar that might have been the near miss of another bullet. The guide's shot had exploded a vertebra to cause instant death.

Telling us about it, Hosea wasn't proud of the achievement. "That grizzly knew I was gunning for him just like the forest ranger had tried to kill him the year before. He was fighting for his life and he knew it." Hosea turned to me with a question: "If you had been the grizzly what would you have done?"

Without waiting for a reply because he was sure what it would have to be, Hosea finished his account of the twenty-fifth bear. He said that night was coming on fast when it was all over. There would be barely time enough to get back to the beach before pitch darkness settled over the wet forest. His partner on the boat would be worried. Turning away from the downed bear, Hosea swung the muzzle of his rifle upward and sent three fast shots crashing through the tree tops. ////

Generation after generation of bears have learned to station themselves directly in the path of leaping salmon.

Bears relish salmon, and feast on it by the ton.

Following pages: **D**ispite their large size, bears are quick and agile on land and in the water.

THEODORE ROOSEVELT

BLACK AND GRIZZLY BEARS

ALTHOUGH IT WAS STILL early in September, the weather was cool and pleasant, the nights being frosty; and every two or three days there was a flurry of light snow, which rendered the labor of tracking much more easy. Indeed, throughout our stay on the mountains, the peaks were snowcapped almost all the time. Our fare was excellent, consisting of elk venison, mountain grouse, and small trout—the last caught in one of the beautiful little lakes that lay almost up by timber line. To us, who had for weeks been accustomed to make small fires from dried brush, or from sage-brush roots, which we dug out of the ground, it was a treat to sit at night before the roaring and crackling pine logs; as the old teamster quaintly put it, we had at last come to a land "where the wood grew on trees." There were plenty of black-tail deer in the woods, and we came across a number of bands of cow and calf elk, or of young bulls; but after several days' hunting we were still without any head worth taking home, and had seen no sign of grizzly, which was the game we were especially anxious to kill; for neither Merrifield nor I had ever seen a wild bear alive.

Sometimes we hunted in company; sometimes each of us went out alone; the teamster, of course, remaining in to guard camp and cook. One day we had separated; I reached camp early in the afternoon, and waited a couple of hours before Merrifield put in an appearance.

At last I heard a shout—the familiar long-drawn *Eikoh-h-h* of the cattlemen,— and he came in sight galloping at speed down an open glade, and waving his

By the end of a good feeding season, a healthy bear will be thick and heavy.

hat, evidently having had good luck; and when he reined in his small, wiry, cow-pony, we saw that he had packed behind his saddle the fine, glossy pelt of a black bear. Better still, he announced that he had been off about ten miles to a perfect tangle of ravines and valleys where bear sign was very thick; and not of black bear either, but of grizzly. The black bear (the only one we got on the mountains) he had run across by accident, while riding up a valley in which there was a patch of dead timber grown up with berry bushes. He noticed a black object which he first took to be a stump; for during the past few days we had each of us made one or two clever stalks up to charred logs, which our imagination converted into bears. On coming near, however, the object suddenly took to its heels; he followed over frightful ground at the pony's best pace, until it stumbled and fell down. By this time he was close on the bear, which had just reached the edge of the wood. Picking himself up, he rushed after it, hearing it growling ahead of him; after running some fifty yards the sound stopped, and he stood still listening. He saw and heard nothing, until he happened to cast his eyes upwards, and there was the bear, almost overhead, and about twenty-five feet up a tree; and in as many seconds afterwards it came down to the ground with a bounce, stone dead. It was a young bear, in its second year, and had probably never before seen a man, which accounted for the ease with which it was treed and taken. One minor result of the encounter was to convince Merrifield—the list of whose faults did not include lack of self-confidence—that he could run down any bear; in consequence of which idea we on more than one subsequent occasion went through a good deal of violent exertion.

Merrifield's tale made me decide to shift camp at once, and go over to the spot where the bear tracks were so plenty. Next morning we were off, and by noon pitched camp by a clear brook, in a valley with steep, wooded sides, but with good feed for the horses in the open bottom. We rigged the canvas wagon-sheet into a small tent, sheltered by the trees from the wind, and piled great pine logs near by where we wished to place the fire; for a night camp in the sharp fall weather is cold and dreary unless there is a roaring blaze of flame in front of the tent. . . .

That evening we almost had a visit from one of the animals we were after. Several times we had heard at night the musical calling of the bull elk—a sound to which no writer has yet done justice. This particular night, when we were in bed and the fire was smoldering, we were roused by a ruder noise—a kind of grunting or roaring whine, answered by the frightened snorts of the ponies. It was a bear which had evidently not seen the fire, as it came from behind the bank, and had probably been attracted by the smell of the horses. After it made out what we were, it stayed round a short while, again uttered its peculiar roaring grunt, and went off; we had seized our rifles and had run out into the woods, but in the darkness could see nothing; indeed, it was rather lucky we did not stumble across the bear, as he could have made short work of us when we were at such a disadvantage.

Next day we went off on a long tramp through the woods and along the sides of the canyons. There were plenty of berry bushes growing in clusters; and all around these there were fresh tracks of bear. But the grizzly is also a flesh-eater, and has a great liking for carrion. On visiting the place where Merrifield had killed the black bear, we found that the grizzlies had been there before us, and had utterly devoured the carcass, with cannibal relish. Hardly a scrap was left, and we turned our steps toward where lay the bull elk I had killed. It was quite late in the afternoon when we reached the place. A grizzly had evidently been at the carcass during the preceding night, for his great footprints were in the ground all around it, and the carcass itself was gnawed and torn, and partially covered with earth and leaves—for the grizzly has a curious habit of burying all of his prey that he does not at the moment need. A great many ravens had been feeding on the body, and they wheeled about over the tree-tops above us, uttering their barking croaks.

The forest was composed mainly of what are called ridge-pole pines, which grow close together, and do not branch out until the stems are thirty or forty feet from the ground. Beneath these trees we walked over a carpet of pine needles, upon which our moccasined feet made no sound. The woods seemed vast and lonely, and their silence was broken now and then by the strange noises always to be heard in the great forests, and which seem to mark the sad and everlasting unrest of the wilderness. We climbed up along the trunk of a dead tree which had toppled over until its upper branches struck in the limb crotch of another, that thus supported it at an angle half-way in its fall. When above the ground far enough to prevent the bear's smelling us, we sat still to wait for his approach; until, in the gathering gloom, we could no longer see the sights of our rifles, and could but dimly make out the carcass of the great elk. It was useless to wait longer; and we clambered down and stole out to the edge of the woods. The forest here covered one side of a steep, almost canyon-like ravine,

whose other side was bare except of rock and sagebrush. Once out from under the trees there was still plenty of light, although the sun had set, and we crossed over some fifty yards to the opposite hillside, and crouched down under a bush to see if, perchance, some animal might not also leave the cover. To our right the ravine sloped downward toward the valley of the Bighorn River, and far on its other side we could catch a glimpse of the great main chain of the Rockies, their snow-peaks glinting crimson in the light of the set sun. Again we waited quietly in the growing dusk until the pine trees in our front blended into one dark, frowning mass. We saw nothing; but the wild creatures of the forest had begun to stir abroad. The owls hooted dismally from the tops of the tall trees, and two or three times a harsh wailing cry, probably the voice of some lynx or wolverine, arose from the depths of the woods. At last, as we were rising to leave, we heard the sound of the breaking of a dead stick from the spot where we knew the carcass lay. It was a sharp, sudden noise, perfectly distinct from the natural creaking and snapping of the branches; just such a sound as would be made by the tread of some heavy creature. "Old Ephraim" had come back to the carcass. A minute afterward, listening with strained ears, we heard him brush by some dry twigs. It was entirely too dark to go in after him; but we made up our minds that on the morrow he should be ours.

Early next morning we were over at the elk carcass, and, as we expected, found that the bear had eaten his full at it during the night. His tracks showed him to be an immense fellow, and were so fresh that we doubted if he had left long before we arrived; and we made up our minds to follow him up and try to find his lair. The bears that lived on these mountains had evidently been little disturbed; indeed, the Indians and most of the white hunters are rather chary of meddling with "Old Ephraim," as the mountain men style the grizzly, unless they get him at a disadvantage; for the sport is fraught with some danger and but small profit. The bears thus seemed to have very little fear of harm, and we thought it likely that the bed of the one who had fed on the elk would not be far away.

My companion was a skillful tracker, and we took up the trail at once. For some distance it led over the soft, yielding carpet of moss and pine needles, and the footprints were quite easily made out, although we could follow them but slowly; for we had, of course, to keep a sharp lookout ahead and around us as we walked noiselessly on in the sombre half-light always prevailing under the great pine trees, through whose thickly interlacing branches stray but few beams of light, no matter how bright the sun may be outside. We made no sound ourselves, and every little sudden noise sent a thrill through me as I peered about with each sense on the alert. Two or three of the ravens that we had scared from the carcass flew overhead, croaking hoarsely; and the pine-tops moaned and sighed in the slight breeze—for pine trees seem to be ever in motion, no matter how light the wind.

After going a few hundred yards the tracks turned off on a well-beaten path made by the elk; the woods were in many places cut up by these game trails, which had often become as distinct as ordinary footpaths. The beast's footprints were perfectly plain in the dust, and he had lumbered along up the path until near the middle of the hillside, where the ground broke away, and there were hollows and boulders. Here there had been a windfall, and the dead trees lay among the living, piled across one another in all directions; while between and around them sprouted up a thick growth of young spruces and other evergreens. The trail turned off into the tangled thicket, within which it was almost certain we would find our quarry. We could still follow the tracks, by the slight scrapes of the claws on the bark, or by the bent and broken twigs; and we advanced with noiseless caution, slowly climbing over the dead tree trunks and upturned stumps, and not letting a branch rustle or catch on our clothes. When in the middle of the thicket we crossed what was almost a breastwork of fallen logs, and Merrifield, who was leading, passed by the upright stem of a great pine. As soon as he was by it, he sank suddenly on one knee, turning half round, his face fairly aflame with excitement; and as I strode past him, with my rifle at the ready, there, not ten steps off, was the great bear, slowly rising from his bed among the young spruces. He had heard us, but apparently hardly knew exactly where or what we were, for he reared up on his haunches sideways to us. Then he saw us, and dropped down again on all fours, the shaggy hair on his neck and shoulders seeming to bristle as he turned toward us. As he sank down on his forefeet I had raised the rifle; his head was bent slightly down, and when I saw the top of the white bead fairly between his small, glittering, evil eyes, I pulled trigger. Half rising up, the huge beast fell over on his side in the death throes, the ball having gone into his brain, striking as fairly between the eyes as if the distance had been measured by a carpenter's rule.

The whole thing was over in twenty seconds from the

time I caught sight of the game; indeed, it was over so quickly that the grizzly did not have time to show fight at all or come a step toward us. It was the first I had ever seen, and I felt not a little proud, as I stood over the great brindled bulk, which lay stretched out at length in the cool shade of the evergreens. He was a monstrous fellow, much larger than any I have seen since, whether alive or brought in dead by the hunters. As near as we could estimate (for of course we had nothing with which to weigh more than very small portions) he must have weighed about 1,200 pounds, and though this is not as large as some of his kind are said to grow in California, it is yet a very unusual size for a bear. . . . He must have been very old, his teeth and claws being all worn down and blunted. . . . He was still in the summer coat, his hair being short, and in color a curious brindled brown. . . .

When the shadows began to lengthen, I shouldered my rifle. . . . Under the dark branches it was already dusk, and the air had the cool chill of evening. ////

Bears till acres of ground in search of the food caches of small mammals and will happily gobble up the mammal too, if they can catch it!

A bear's thick fur often masks its true size.

Following pages: **T**he plentiful food supply of Alaskan salmon streams makes competition less necessary and affords a moment of companionable relaxation.

THE BLACK GRIZZLY

BY LATE AFTERNOON THE snow melted and I had not seen a thing. I started breaking down my camera, getting ready to return to the Hilton, when I heard movement in the brush below me to the north. The sow with the dark patch on her hump, from the previous night, and her small, light-colored cub walked onto the false hellebore-studded meadow near the snowfield. The cub leapt and nipped at its mother, who wanted no part of the play. She was clearly nervous. The cub paused to graze on the low sedges growing on the wet flats below the snow, then ran to catch up to the sow, who had started climbing the long ridge between me and the Grizzly Hilton. She would pass over the saddle just in front of me. I did not want to disturb the grizzly family, but I did not want to be stuck on the ridge after dark either.

I decided to let the bears pass over the ridge first, then slip by them and climb the rest of the way to the Hilton. If I was careful, they would not get my scent.

Darkness was falling and the grizzlies had not hit the ridge top yet—they had stopped to feed on huckleberries. I was waiting in the shadows when my heart skipped a couple of beats: below, in the meadow, stood the Black Grizzly, nibbling sedge. I hoped he would stay down there. I already had two grizzlies between me and my camp, and it would be dark in forty-five minutes.

The Black Grizzly crossed the meadow with his usual disdain for scents and worlds beyond his immediate one and started browsing his way up the side of the ridge. He climbed rapidly and was halfway up the ridge

It is easy to understand why Native American tribes have developed a rich and diverse set of beliefs about the bear as a spiritual presence.

when it dawned on me that he was going to catch up to the grizzly family feeding just below me. I was going to be stuck there in the dark with a sow, her cub, and the Black Grizzly between me and my sleeping bag. I edged off to the side of the steep-sided ridge to get a better view. The Black Grizzly browsed a hundred feet or so below the sow; neither bear seemed aware of the other. I considered dropping off the back side of the ridge and trying to circle around the three bears, but I would never make it; the steep brush was nearly impenetrable.

Suddenly there was a roar, and I heard a huffing and the sound of animals running through the brush. The sow broke into the open a hundred feet in front of me and raced across the saddle. The tiny cub struggled with the brush, running at her heels. I could hear the intake and exhalation of each breath with each stride. They contoured along the rock outcrop below the ridge, oblivious of my presence, running for their lives before the Black Grizzly, who tore up the slope and burst over the ridge top. He galloped like a racehorse and moved just as fast. The sow and cub flew below the small cliff. The cub fell a couple of yards behind and I could make out a high-pitched coughing, a panicky sound as if the little bear knew it had but seconds left to live. The Black Grizzly gained ground until his jaws were but a yard from the cub's hindquarters.

At the last second the sow spun on her heels, allowing the cub to slip under her as she braced for the crush of the huge grizzly with a chilling roar. The boar bellowed back, and they locked jaws. The Black Grizzly slashed with his teeth. The sow parried and warded off the attacking jaws of the bigger bear. The cub

retreated to a rock thirty feet above and stood there bawling. The boar leapt forward and knocked the smaller sow offbalance, forcing her to expose her vulnerable flank. The huge male lunged and seized the female by the neck. She yelped in pain, throwing her head against the bigger bear, and broke the grip of his jaws. The sow quickly recovered. She held her own.

I could see no blood, though both bears must have been wounded by then. They alternately slashed and parried, then stood nose to nose roaring amplified growls, the likes of which I had never heard in nature. The Black Grizzly slowed his attack. Abruptly he changed tactics and lunged once again for the throat of the sow. She leaned into the attack; they locked jaws and rose to their hind feet like circling wrestlers. They broke and dropped to all fours, roaring and bellowing into each other's snouts.

The face-off stabilized as the Black Grizzly gave up trying to kill the sow. The last roars rumbled throughout the valley. Though a little shaken by the proximity of this battle, I managed to run a few feet of film.

The smaller of the two huge carnivores backed slowly up the hill, still growling with the hair on her neck straight up. The Black Grizzly roared again, his head slightly lowered, his ears flattened back. She inched away from him a few feet at a time and turned her head to the side—a sign she was done fighting. He read it and turned away almost regretfully. The battle was over.

I was in a predicament. It was almost dark and I was perched on a knife-edged ridge with steep, impassable brush on either side and nowhere to go but up to the Grizzly Hilton. Between me and the Hilton, one hundred and fifty feet away, stood the baddest bear in the mountains, now at his ugliest after an inconclusive fight.

I let my instincts loose: I had no choice but to face down the great grizzly. Any failure of confidence could be fatal. I picked up two large brown bags that had been covering my camera and held them at arm's length. I was wearing a black sweater; both black and dark brown grizzlies were often big males. The Black Grizzly turned just off the crest of the ridge a hundred feet away and pretended to feed. He still had not seen me.

I made my move. Slowly I inched up the ridge and spoke. "Hey, grizzer bear, it's only me, good old Arapaho. Sure hate to bother you." The words were irrelevant, but tone and posture were everything. The grizzly reared and spun. He took a huge breath, exhaled like a sounding whale, then dropped to all fours facing me. I continued inching toward him, my arms outstretched holding the silly garbage bags, talking nonsense with my head cocked off to the side. The grizzly clicked and gnashed his teeth. I stopped at fifty feet and the bear advanced stiff-legged toward me. His ears were flat back against his head. I was finished. "I'll make it up to you, griz, honest." At fifteen feet away the great bear stopped, his head lowered. There was something in his eyes that I would never quite put my finger on. The Black Grizzly turned his head to the side, almost sadly, spun gracefully on his rear feet, and ambled off into the brush leaving me alone on the ridge top.

Only half believing my good fortune, I wasted no time. I slid by the spot where the bear disappeared and shot up the ridge to my hilltop camp. By the time I got there it was dark. I leaned into the darkness listening for sounds and caught myself shaking uncontrollably. The last time I had shaken like this was 1967 near Ba An, after my Montagnards and I had been strafed by gunships flying for the 101st Airborne.

Normally I build no fires at the Grizzly Hilton because I don't like to spook the bears, but that night a fire was my only defense against the roaming bear I had just escaped. I worked fast, kindling a tiny blaze a few feet from my hidden tent. The fire bolstered my shaky nerves, and I stepped to the edge of the hill. Somewhere, down in the darkness, was the unmistakable sound of a big animal moving through the brush. I listened breathlessly. The Black Grizzly was coming uphill. I stoked up the fire and gathered beargrass plumes. I made a torch of them, but the stalks burned poorly. I added branches and got the whole thing flaming. I heard the snapping of brush just over the edge of the knoll. Again, I had no choice but confrontation. Walking to the brink of the hill, I heard the grizzly moving not forty feet downslope. I spoke softly, telling the bear I was sorry that I had invaded his territory, thanking him, and assuring him I would move on. Waving the flaming plumes and branches in the air, I saw the small eyes shine red for a second. They blinked off and disappeared into the darkness. I heard the huge bear slowly move through the bushes back down the hill. I went back and huddled by the fire.

Half an hour passed, maybe more. I was beginning to think the bear would leave me in peace when I heard thrashing in the shrub field on the other side of the knoll. Again I gathered firebrands and walked to the edge of the steep drop-off. I stared into the darkness and heard the angry grizzly fight his way up the hill. When he got thirty feet away, I threw a burning branch down the slope. The bear stopped. I waved the brands in the air and said, "Hey, Black Grizzly, it's me again. Why don't you give me a break?"

Silence. I peered into the blackness, seeing nothing. The torch had almost burned down, leaving me unprotected. The big bear slowly withdrew down the mountain. An hour later I heard him probe the third side of the pyramid-shaped hill. The scene was repeated.

The wind rose, bringing dim sounds of dark shapes to my ears. The snapping of a twig carried to the fire, and my head jerked toward the black trees, finding nothing. It must have been midnight. I could not remember being so tired. I could not afford to fall asleep. I tried to keep my mind moving. My thoughts drifted, landing on the irony of meeting my end at the jaws of my favorite beast. For a moment I could imagine the flickering fire reflecting the hint of a smile on my face. It vanished as I heard another branch break.

By about two in the morning, peace returned to the mountains, broken only once by bugling elk in a distant basin. I dozed by my tiny fire, waking every half hour to rekindle a small blaze. Gray dawn broke in the southeastern sky. With each moment the daylight spread and my confidence returned. Still I had to get out of these hills, past the Black Grizzly.

I picked up my binoculars and walked to the edge of the knoll where I could see down onto the basin. A couple of hundred yards to my right the brown grizzly with her two lovely blond yearlings ate berries. She sniffed the air and trotted away from me. Shit, she got my scent. The bears ambled through the steep brush, then picked up a near-vertical bear trail leading to the bottom of the basin.

In the trees near the edge of the sedge meadow I saw a dark shape. The Black Grizzly stepped into the open and began grazing. The sow and her two yearlings continued dropping down the steep trail. Just as they hit the bottom, the big boar lifted his head and saw the family a hundred yards away across the flat. Without pausing, he charged full tilt over the log-filled meadow. The sow and her young turned, scrambled back up the steep game trail, and climbed above a rocky outcrop out on a low cliff. The Black Grizzly stopped at the foot of the hill and looked up, allowing the family to reach safety on the cliffs.

Another close one.

I was upset with myself. I had almost run those little bears into that black bastard and got them killed. That's it, I'm leaving as soon as he beds. I was angry at the Black Grizzly for being such a cantankerous son of a bitch, but he was just being a bear. I was a blundering nuisance who was not doing the bears a bit of good.

I hiked back to camp in the afternoon to finish packing up. The bears should have been bedded by now. I approached the Grizzly Hilton and stopped short. Something was wrong. Down stuffing covered everything. My cache of gear had been pulled down from the tree and the contents scattered. My sleeping bag was torn to shreds. I found my dirty brown T-shirt chewed to pieces. The bear had eaten everything that smelled of me.

I packed up the remains of my camp, threw it in the backpack, and started down the ridge. I glassed the timber just below the basin and caught a flash of the black bear on his daybed. He was so arrogant he did not even bother hiding in the timber like other bears. I could see half of his enormous body stretched out in the open.

I approached my observation post with apprehension. Two of my one-gallon water canteens lay on the ground crushed by the grizzly's jaws. The camera and the tripod were knocked over. The foam sound blimp had been chewed off Gage's old Bolex, which, outside of a few canine dents, was undamaged.

I stuffed my pack with damaged equipment, trembling slightly out of mixed rage and fear. I walked the ridge to the spot directly over the Black Grizzly's daybed. I pried loose the biggest boulder I could find and rolled it down the slope, crashing into the timber. The great bear lifted his head and looked up at me. A piercing cry shattered the silence as I roared at him. He yawned and his head disappeared again in the thick trees. I turned and slipped on down the ridge, leaving the bear and the mountains behind. ////

Bears are the consummate opportunistic feeders. Their survival strategy includes a willingness to eat almost anything.

Although grizzly bears in the northern Rockies are thought of as open-country animals, most of their time is spent in or along the edge of the forest.

The mother bear's protectiveness is legendary and yet, if necessary, she will abandon the cubs to save her own life. If she lives, she can have other cubs, but if she dies, her genetic line ends.

A *bear's thick fur provides isolation from the elements and protection against pests and the claws of other predators.*

AN ORIGINAL ESSAY BY

MARK SPRAGG

ADOPTING BEAR

I WAS RAISED ON THE national forest that drops off the eastern plateau of Yellowstone Park and so bear, mostly grizzlies, were part of my boyhood. I did not think of them entirely as animals, but as older, wilder boys; as a pack of savvy bullies that prowled my neighborhood. They were my heroes. I wished to grow up to be a bear; I wished to stand in the space between our species. I longed to roam the mountains with their impunity, to earn their acceptance, to learn the language of bear. Being merely a boy seemed restricting.

I envied them their power, their speed, knew them to be faster than our fastest horse, understood that they could usually scent me more accurately than I could sight them. I was fully aware that if I was unlucky, or uncareful, that a bear might kill me. I knew Smokey was a cartoon and not the real item. I did not confuse the two. I envisioned bear as big, proud, atavistic brothers seated at the head of the table in a very real food chain in which I represented a lesser part. I took it on faith that if I ate quietly and reverently that I would be tolerated.

The only man I knew who ate at the bear's end of the table was an aged trapper. He visited occasionally to see people and to tell his story. He kept the trophy of a Zippo lighter, its center punctured perfectly by a grizzly's tooth. The hole was bigger than my thickest finger.

Once he dropped his pants to show me a misshapen thigh grown back mostly hairless in scar tissue. The lighter had been in his jeans pocket on the day a bear had bitten into him, shook him like a juvenile

Because the bear's eyesight is perhaps the weakest of its senses, it relies on a keen sense of smell and hearing.

marmot, and pitched him down a hundred yards of scree slope and sudden drops. He had been tasted by bear and it made him, in my estimation, superior to other men. I imagined him part of my bloodline. I fantasized him as a secret grandfather.

It was a fantasy largely engendered by the shame I felt for my family's outfitting business. My father, as a professional hunter and guide, openly advertised the deaths of bear, and because of that commerce I stood away from him when out of the house, not wanting by association to become an enemy of bear. Trying, in fact, to adopt the mannerisms of the old trapper.

There are few satisfying explanations for why we love, and I still have no reason for my love of bear. Because I was too cowardly to try to live with them—too hapless to be mauled—they came to me in my dreams. I have for almost forty years had a recurrent dream of bear. I consider it their gift to me. Bear have embraced me in my dreams.

The first dead bear I saw was skinned and his naked body so remarkably like that of a large man's that I thought there'd been an accident. It was like looking at John Wayne having fallen getting out of a bath. I thought I might vomit, but then my horse scented the corpse, shied, and threw me. They could not drag my horse or me near the bloody thing.

Still today when I conjure bear I experience a sense of vertigo, my mouth waters, and I flush. I feel on the verge of accident.

When I was ten one of our hired hands drove me to a land-fill in Yellowstone in the middle of the night. We sat in his pickup with the lights and heater on and watched twenty grizzlies scrabble for the choicer bits of garbage. It was a degraded scene, and had for me the demoralizing effect of being made to sit in a bar packed with one's aunts and uncles become loud, bloated, drunk, and dangerous. I squinted hard to blur the scene in an effort to more easily imagine them as something else, as a swarm of behemoth bees on some ruined blossom of refuse. Not bear. It was a trick to keep me also from crying, to keep my notions of them unsoiled. To find this clan of savages capable of addiction left me desolate.

For most of the years we outfitted my father hired an old and voluble man as his camp cook. He was uncommonly skinny, rheumy, and his fear of bear ran more deeply than anyone I knew. He was evangelistic in his hatred of them, slandered them at every opportunity, and I loathed him.

He slept on a pole bench built into the rear of the cook tent—a roomy affair with five-foot sidewalls and a ridgepole that the tallest of us could not reach on our best jumps. It was big enough for the old cook, the food panniers, for a half dozen men to stand thawing in front of the cook stove. My point is to give you a sense of the proportions of the tent.

On a night late into the third hunt a grizzly swung through our camp, stood on the log rolled to the back of the tent, stretched up to its apex, and ripped down the entire wall. None of us saw the actual event, but we heard the immediate screams of the cook, rolled out of our own tents, running toward the sound of him, running partially clothed and unhappy about having to dive into the snow under a barrage of gunfire.

The old man spun inside the ruined tent, shooting a high-caliber rifle into the air as fast as his shaking hands would allow.

The shots were high and uncommonly effective in destroying the canvas meant to be its roof. I had never seen a rifle shot at night and was amazed at how far the flames licked out of its muzzle.

When he emptied the magazine two men subdued him before he could reload, and the rest of us lit lanterns. I was the only one who thought the incident hilarious, and was barely smart enough hide my happiness. I walked a little into the timber, smirking, and held my light down to see the size of the bear's tracks stamped into the snow. I bit the insides of my cheeks. Each paw print looked large enough to drop a good-sized dog through. I considered it obvious that the bear had come as a vigilante, but leniently; the incident meant as a warning for the cook to keep his mouth shut.

On the last hunt that year a guide was badly mauled. He lived, but the thirty-mile ride out of camp was truly torturous. This man I exalted as a saint; not only tasted by bear, but generous enough to take on the cook's karma.

When I was fourteen I was ordered to become a traitor to bear. I was sent with a guide to track a big, dish-faced grizzly one of our hunters had managed to wound: an apprenticeship for which I did not volunteer. The guide was thickly muscled, in his prime, a huge man, but when given the job of tracking the bear— with me as his backup—became obviously pale and began to drool. I sulked and hoped that he might be overcome by a seizure.

I waited with the man past what he reckoned was long enough for the bear to sicken and want to die and then reluctantly set off with him. The first mile or so was through an area that had burned twenty years earlier, and was then grown woolly with spruce seven to eight feet high. So thick, in fact, that we had to part the bows with our rifle barrels to step ahead. Any sound, real or imagined, sent the man stampeding back over the top of me. I was not a big boy; hardly made him lose his balance. Before we reached more open country my head, shoulders, and chest had been stomped a dozen times. I lagged back enough to dodge his retreats, and dabbed at my wounds while one eye swelled shut. I prayed that the damage done me would be seen as adequate penance for my participation. I prayed for redemption short of actually being eaten.

The blood trail stopped in a seep where the bear had lain to cool himself and pack his wounds with mud. He then climbed an escarpment so steep that we had to strap our rifles on our backs to follow. When we reached the top and had gone another mile on level ground we found his stride lengthening and we turned back hoping to reach camp before dark. The man said that he would start again in the morning, but that the sign looked to be that of a bear growing healthy.

Halfway back we found new track. On top of ours. The bear had circled and was tracking us. I'm certain he watched us home, perhaps advancing as close as a dozen yards, and I still do not know why he did not kill us, exact some revenge. We had, of course, wronged him, damaged him for some idiot sense of trophy. He let me live, but took away my dreams of bear.

I was desperate that bear not abandon me altogether, and in an attempt at vindication—later that winter with my brother's help—untacked a bear rug from our father's wall, pulled it over our backs, and rushed into the cabin where the big tracker sat on his bed picking his toes. When we lowered the hide, grinning, expecting to be cuffed, he was gone. We stared through a torn screen, down at him writhing on the ground, around the pain of a broken arm. To his credit he did not shriek. He simply stood and dove through the handiest window.

We sneaked away and swore a pact of silence. Privately, I think it occurred to the man, probably after he was airborne, that he was the butt of a prank. In that he never spoke of the incident as anything but a genuine assassination attempt allowed him to maintain his prestige as a man eminently worthy of attack. One is, after all, judged by the strength of one's enemies. My dreams of bear returned to me that night.

I have tried always to keep bear friendly in my heart. But, I have never known how to make them fully my brethren. I was raised to hunt them, and stink of that guilt and ignorance. Saying I'm sorry seems simply puny.

I hunt nothing now, have never hunted for trophy, but lived my boyhood among bear, and rubbed up against them as an immature and degenerate predator. I feel that it is the result of those early crimes, that I have matured afraid of bear. They have become a foreign thing to me, they have become beasts, and I fear that they will kill me if caught out on their country.

This winter I walked out into the mountains on its coldest day. The snow squealed under my feet as an animal would squeal penned for slaughter. I had come into the mountains to remember bear. I chose the temperature to remember them starkly. My shadow dropped away from me as gray as gunmetal.

I gained some altitude and squinted into the winter landscape. My eyelashes froze to one another. I blinked continually to see at all. My nostrils froze to the post of my nose and I breathed shallowly through my mouth, careful not to frost my lungs; to chill myself from the inside out. Ice formed heavily in my mustache and beard.

The sky was one primary blue. It was well below zero and the air glittered crystalline with minute particles of ice so light they would not fall, but danced the landscape alive, announcing the cold profound.

The mountains were quietly held white with snow, the evergreens muted vaguely blue-green. The creeks worked over their smooth beds of stone, invisibly under a mottled foot of ice. The chokecherry and rose hips were desiccated beads of hard color only, scattered among their naked branches, the brush willow left as leafless spikes of soft ocher. For fifty miles in every direction it was January and the earth was pounded silent. It was a day as deadly and beautiful as my memories of bear. They were out around me. Buried in their dens across the mountain latitudes, in every direction from me were the blood-warm burrows of bear.

The big boars curl languidly to sleep, shifting to scratch and smack their jowls. The sows, filled with milk, winter their fatness against the appetites of their cubs. In this landscape where nearly all of their prey struggle to keep the engines of their bodies warmed against death—in a race with spring to simply stay alive— the bear sleep like fierce and patient sidhas feeding on the fat of feasts they made in better weather. They have adapted to these forests, to this slant of planet that our sun warms weakly through the darker solstice. Nothing hunts them, but us. They are neighbors with everything but man. We have overmatched their predations. We have, as one example, unhinged the souls of sixty million bison. While they feed on berries, fish, rodents, and the crippled, the slow, the aged, and unwary young of ungulates, we kill the best of them, the chiefs of their race. Their only peace comes in sleep beneath the snow.

I walked forward imagining their breaths. I imagined it rising, condensing in slim spires, like little flues, from their quiet homes. I asked for forgiveness for my crimes against them, aware that I am only fully brave to walk among them while they sleep.

That night I dreamed my dream of bear. It happens more often as I age, its text always remains the same, and is the only evidence that I once loved them. I sit in the lap of huge, blubbery sow. She is like the Venus of Willendorf with brown and golden hair, with claws, with teats that drip a rich, white milk. She wraps her arms around me and she rocks from side to side. Together we watch a deep, green river move in front of us, and I feel strong and as though I might be her young and naked son.

Sometimes I wake at night and smell her breath. It is hot and foul and smells of wildness. I think sometimes that she is my death. Come for me. Or come to make a truce, to teach me to be again unafraid of bear, to live what life I have more lightly, and less timid. She comes to hold me tight, to grasp me to her strength and dignity. To convince me to walk in the forest aware that I too will die, reduce to earth, and if I am fortunate, return to live with the grace of bear. ////

Following pages: **W**hile keeping low for cover, a bear will rear up for a better look when catching a scent or hearing a sound.